A
Disturbance
in
Mirrors

Recent Titles in
Contributions in Women's Studies

A
DISTURBANCE
IN
MIRRORS

The Poetry of Sylvia Plath

Pamela J. Annas

CONTRIBUTIONS IN WOMEN'S STUDIES,
NUMBER 89

GREENWOOD PRESS

New York • Westport, Connecticut • London

Library of Congress Cataloging-in-Publication Data

Annas, Pamela J.
    A disturbance in mirrors.

    (Contributions in women's studies, ISSN 0147-104X ;
no. 89)
    Bibliography: p.
    Includes index.
    1. Plath, Sylvia—Criticism and interpretation.
2. Plath, Sylvia—Style. I. Title. II. Series.
PS3566.L27Z564   1988   811'.54   87-23653
ISBN 0-313-24997-0 (lib. bdg. : alk. paper)

British Library Cataloguing in Publication Data is available.

Library of Congress Catalog Card Number: 87-23653
ISBN: 0-313-24997-0
ISSN: 0147-104X

First published in 1988

Greenwood Press, Inc.
88 Post Road West, Westport, Connecticut 06881

Printed in the United States of America

The paper used in this book complies with the
Permanent Paper Standard issued by the National
Information Standards Organization (Z39.48-1984).

10 9 8 7 6 5 4 3 2

❧ Contents ❧

A
Disturbance
in
Mirrors

❧ 1 ❧

Reflections

I sought my image
   in the scorching glass,
for what fire could damage
   a witch's face?

"On Looking into the
Eyes of a Demon Lover"
(n.d.)

From the mercury-backed glass
Mother, grandmother, greatgrandmother
Reach hag hands to haul me in,
And an image looms under the fishpond surface
Where the daft father went down
With orange duck-feet winnowing his hair—

"All the Dead Dears" (1957)

Nobody watched me before, now I am watched.
The tulips turn to me, and the window behind me
Where once a day the light slowly widens and slowly thins,
And I see myself, flat, ridiculous, a cut-paper shadow
Between the eye of the sun and the eyes of the tulips,
And I have no face, I have wanted to efface myself.
The vivid tulips eat my oxygen.

"Tulips" (1961)

The heart shuts,
The sea slides back,
The mirrors are sheeted.

"Contusion" (1963)

From her early poems to her last, the mirror is a recurrent and powerful image for Sylvia Plath. It gathers together a number of her central themes: her exploration of the boundary between self and world, her struggle to be reborn into a transformed world, her concern with what is true and what is false, what is real and what is unreal, her interest in the process of perception and creation, her self-consciousness and above all, her ambivalence. In the mirror Plath tries on the various guises, masks, avatars, personae of her poems—witch, mermaid, lover, wife; mushroom, dead mole, grain of rice; mother, daughter, barren woman, fertile woman, dead woman; hospital patient, beekeeper, poet, and vengeful goddess. The mirror is the central image of a cluster of reflecting images—crystal ball, eye, moon, mirage, bell jar, window, shadow, balloon, polished stone, and the sea—which suggest potentiality and constraint, sometimes both at once.

The mirror is never an entirely comfortable image for Plath, as the four quotations at the beginning of this chapter indicate. The mirror stands for an undefined and dangerously shifting area of uncertainty and tension. The mirror eyes of her demon lover are filled with flames; only by taking on the otherworldly identity of witch and giving up her identity as human woman can she survive unscathed. In "All the Dead Dears," both reflecting surfaces—literal mirror and pond—become transparent and reveal another and threatening world behind them, which will either pull her in (in the case of her mother) or beckon her under the surface to drown (in the case of her father). Again, she will be forced to give up her identity as a separate person as she is immersed in their behind-the-mirror and underwater reality. In "Tulips," as a convalescent hospital patient, the speaker of the poem is already at a low ebb of vitality, though the poem is about the process of recovery. Embarrassed and self-conscious, she is doubly reflected: In the mirror of the window she sees herself flat, papery, and two-dimensional, caught between two mirrors—the eye of the sun and the eyes of the vivid red tulips. She wants to efface herself, become no face at all, in order to escape the perplexity of too many reflections and too many expectations hooking her back into life. While in "Tulips" her heart "opens and closes / Its bowl of red blooms out of sheer love of me," in "Contusion" "the heart shuts" and the sea's mirrors are "sheeted," suggesting a house that is being closed for the season. The image also suggests an end to the movement, however terrifying, unsettling, and circular, that the mirrors have at least allowed.

Sylvia Plath's mirrors demonstrate the process of self and world meeting and indicate the location at which they meet. "Cold glass, how you insert yourself / Between myself and myself" ("The Other," 1962). The mirror is a tricky, untrustworthy, confusing, alternately rigid and insubstantial boundary between self and world, self and self. In Lewis Carroll's *Through the Looking Glass*, Alice, whom Plath in an early poem refers to as "my muse Alice," climbed through the mirror into another world. Sylvia Plath too often found herself up on the mantelpiece touching her hands to the glass and wondering whether to pass through, catching glimpses of a world as strange as but far less full of delight than the world Alice saw. She balanced on the border between two worlds and wrote about what she saw from that privileged and precarious position, not as wondering and innocent Alice but as Gerd, the crystal gazer, who "craved / To govern more sight than given to a woman / By wits alone" ("Crystal Gazer," 1956).

There are these possible fates for the person who looks in mirrors, and they recur throughout Plath's poetry in various ways: (1) you may, like Medusa who saw herself, see something in the mirror that turns you into stone and locks you rigidly into an identity; (2) you may pass through the boundary of the mirror and dissolve, losing a separate identity; (3) you may, caught between two mirrors, see only a shimmering and infinite series of reflections and never have the question of identity resolved; (4) you may see nothing at all, and that is death.

"Family Reunion" and "Moonsong at Morning," both written before 1956, end with the speaker counseling death by water. In "Family Reunion" she writes, "I cast off my identity / And make the fatal plunge"; in "Moonsong at Morning," a poem addressed to the moon, she ends,

> Reflect in terror
> The scorching sun:
> dive at your mirror
> and drown within.

"Ouija" (1957) posits "a chilly god, a god of shades," who "rises to the glass from his black fathoms." "Lorelei" and "Full Fathom

Five" (both 1958) see shapes below the surface that the speaker of the poems wants to join. In a 1961 poem, "Mirror," the mirror is swallowing images, eating time: "In me she has drowned a young girl, and in me an old woman / Rises toward her day after day, like a terrible fish." In "Crossing the Water" (1962), "stars open among the lilies. / Are you not blinded by such expressionless sirens? / This is the silence of astounded souls."

A number of the personae of Plath's poems are caught between mirrors, not sure what is real or significant and what is illusion. "Sleep in the Mojave Desert" (1960) centers on mirages, "those glittery fictions of spilt water / That glide ahead of the very thirsty." While the speaker of "Tulips" has no face, in the head of the "Insomniac" (1961) "is a little interior of gray mirrors. / Each gesture flees immediately down an alley / Of diminishing perspectives, and its significance / Drains like water out the hole at the far end." In her verse play, *Three Women* (1962), Plath's second voice (the Secretary, who loses her child) says ironically as she leaves the hospital: "The mirror gives back a woman without deformity. / The nurses give back my clothes, and an identity." In "A Birthday Present" (1962), Plath writes: "Let us sit down to it, one on either side, admiring the gleam / The glaze, the mirrory variety of it. / Let us eat our last supper at it, like a hospital plate." After asking her "applicant" if he wears a glass eye, Plath says, doubling the reflection:

> You have a hole, it's a poultice.
> You have an eye, it's an image.
> My boy, it's your last resort.
> Will you marry it, marry it, marry it.
>
> "The Applicant" (1962)

Shattered or defective mirrors appear in "Thalidomide" (1962), "The Couriers" (1962), and "Words" (1963). In "Thalidomide," "The glass cracks across, / The image / Flees and aborts like dropped mercury." In "Words," Plath speaks of the ineffectuality of words both as "dry and riderless" hoof taps and as "Water striving / To re-establish its mirror / Over the rock." Finally, in "The Couriers," "A ring of gold with the sun in it? / Lies. Lies and a grief" is a false sign and is set against these lines, a true sign, which end the poem: "A disturbance in mirrors, / The sea shattering its gray one. / Love, love, my season."

Plath's fascination with mirror imagery began early and consciously, perhaps as a way of imaging her own ambivalence and sense of division. Her senior honors thesis at Smith College, written in 1954–1955, the year following her suicide attempt and recovery, was called "The Magic Mirror: A Study of the Double in Two of Dostoevsky's Novels." In the introduction, she writes:

the appearance of the Double is an aspect of man's eternal desire to solve the enigma of his own identity. By seeking to read the riddle of his soul in its myriad manifestations, man is brought face to face with his own mysterious mirror image, an image which he confronts with mingled curiosity and fear. This simultaneous attraction and repulsion arises from the inherently ambivalent nature of the Double, which may embody not only good, creative characteristics, but also evil, destructive ones.[1]

After discussing examples of the double in Poe, Stevenson, and Wilde, she remarks: "The confrontation of the Double in these instances usually results in a duel which ends in insanity or death for the original hero."[2] Plath bases her study of the image of the double in Dostoevsky on Otto Rank's work and other investigations into the schizophrenic personality. Her discussion of motifs in *The Double* might be a prescient description of motifs in her own subsequent poetry; she writes that the motifs that "illustrate Godyakin's dilemma . . . include the repetition of mirror imagery, identification with animals, and a simultaneous fear of murder and desire for death."[3] Plath concludes her 60-page thesis with these remarks:

It is Godyakin's inability to *acknowledge* his inner conflict and Ivan's inability to *reconcile* his inner conflict which result in severe schizophrenia for both. . . . Dostoevsky implies that recognition of our various mirror images and reconciliation with them will save us from disintegration. This reconciliation does not mean a simple or monolithic resolution of conflict, but rather a creative acknowledgement of the fundamental duality of man; it involves a constant courageous acceptance of the eternal paradoxes within the universe and within ourselves.[4]

Much of Sylvia Plath's poetry springs from her own attempts to recognize and reconcile her own paradoxes, the ones she found inside herself and the ones she faced in the world she lived in. Like the work of a number of twentieth-century women poets, Sylvia Plath's poetry can be characterized as a search not so much for definition of self as for redefinition of self. The dialectic of Plath's poetry is, first, the tension between a self-defined self and an other-defined self, and second, the tension between the self-image of the poet and the poet's image of society. The poems examine the relationship between a divided and alienated self and a contradictory and alienating world; the contradictions and the alienation increase as Plath's mythologizing of her images of self and world changes from natural and supernatural in the early poems to social and historical in the late poems. As Sylvia Plath increasingly places herself within a social context, one that is historical and linear rather than natural and cyclical, she begins to see herself as trapped. In "The Moon and the Yew Tree" (1961) she says, "I simply cannot see where there is to get to." The self is caught between stasis and process, isolation and engagement, objectivity and subjectivity, speech and silence, and the search for a self reborn into a reborn world occurs in conflict, between the twin mirrors of the world and her own mind.

I began working on this book in the mid 1970s, the year after I introduced a course on Contemporary Women Poets at Indiana University. I had been impressed then by the strong reaction of women students to Sylvia Plath's work; their responses to Plath's poems were of an entirely different order than those to the work of the three other women poets we read—Anne Sexton, Denise Levertov, and Diane Wakoski. Plath's poems struck them in a way that provoked shock, hostility, or a dangerous identification with the personae of her poems. Certainly the poems drew from them an energy which went far beyond the usual response to readings assigned in an upper-level literature class and ranged from stunned silence and tears after hearing a tape recording of Plath reading "Daddy" and "Lady Lazarus" through brilliant papers to late night telephone calls from students who had also contemplated suicide. My sense now is that Plath's writing captured the anger, the self-doubt, and the ambivalence that many intelligent and creative women were experiencing in the late 1960s and early 1970s as they became aware of the discrepancies between the potential they had begun to glimpse in themselves and the constraining definitions of women's capacities that they encountered daily in the world and certainly in literature courses at most universities—which by and large ignored women poets.

Virginia Woolf said in *A Room of One's Own* that "a woman writing thinks back through her mothers" and that women novelists in the nineteenth century had the bare minimum of a female tradition with which to identify.[5] The position of a woman poet in the middle of the twentieth century was perhaps more problematic, for she faced a much longer and more established tradition of poetry as a high art shaped primarily by male poets. "The language most emphatically denied to women," writes Cora Kaplan in "Language and Gender," is the most concentrated form of symbolic language—poetry."[6] Cheryl Walker, in *The Nightingale's Burden*, discusses the woman poet's ambivalence toward her own creativity and power and categorizes poems as "identifications with power, identifications with powerlessness, and reconciling poems that attempt to establish a ground for power in the midst of powerlessness itself."[7] She says that American women poets have been ambivalent "toward the desire for power, toward their ambitions, toward their need to say 'I am' boldly and effectively in the creative world" and that this "reflects women's uncertain standing in the patriarchal world."[8] Though Walker is here talking about Anne Bradstreet, who wrote three hundred years before Sylvia Plath, I sense the same kind of ambivalence in Plath's poems and private writings toward her own power as a woman and a poet.

Here is one way in which that ambivalence is expressed. Though Plath speaks admiringly of male poets—William Butler Yeats, T. S. Eliot, e. e. cummings, W. H. Auden, Archibald Macleish, Conrad Aiken—she saw herself as part of a tradition of women poets and reserved her overt feelings of competitiveness for other contemporary women poets. She writes in her journal:

Arrogant, I think I have written lines which qualify me to be The Poetess of America (as Ted will be the Poet of England and her dominions). Who rivals? Well, in history Sappho, Elizabeth Barrett Browning, Christina Rossetti, Amy Lowell, Emily Dickinson, Edna St. Vincent Millay—all dead. Now: Edith Sitwell and Marianne Moore, the aging giantesses, and poetic godmother Phyllis McGinley is out—light verse: she's sold herself.

Rather: May Swenson, Isabella Gardner, and most close, Adrienne Cecile Rich—who will soon be eclipsed by these eight poems: I am eager, chafing, sure of my gift, wanting only to train and teach it—I'll count the magazines and money I break open by these eight best poems from now on. We'll see.[9]

In a time previous to women's presses and poetry magazines, I think Plath was aware that there was only so much space in the world of published poetry for women poets, that she was seen as a woman poet, and that her competitors for space in print were other women poets. She may also not have wanted to feel competitive with her husband, Ted Hughes. In addition, Plath and the other mid-twentieth century women poets with whom she felt compared were all confronting a long and overwhelmingly male tradition of poetry whose concerns, images, and language were not necessarily the same as theirs. They were writing for an audience with certain expectations about what a poem was; what its subject matter appropriately was; what was serious, powerful, and significant and what was hysterical, trivial, and dismissable. These poets, including Plath, must have felt considerable conflict as they mediated between what they needed to say and what was considered sayable.

When I began to read the early criticism of Sylvia Plath's work, I found a range of critical responses which indicated that trained literary critics were, like my students, reeling under the impact of Plath's poetry—her saying of the unsayable—and were handling their responses in a variety of ways. One early round of criticism apotheosized Sylvia Plath into a contemporary myth. Robert Lowell is symptomatic in his foreword to the American edition of *Ariel* when he writes that "Sylvia Plath becomes herself—hardly a person at all, or a woman, certainly not another 'poetess,' but one of those super-real, hypnotic great classical heroines."[10] A. Alvarez, in *The Savage God: A Study of Suicide*, picking up one of Lowell's phrases, suggests that Plath was conditioned and compelled by the subject matter of her poetry to play a dangerous game, a kind of "Russian roulette," with her life in the name of her art.[11] Robin Morgan in her poem "Arraignment" accused Ted Hughes of murder and made Plath a kind of super victim and feminist martyr.[12] Many of the early critics of Plath's poetry took the fact of her suicide as a starting point and interpreted the poetry in the light of that event. Another approach is exemplified by M. L. Rosenthal, who grouped Plath with Anne Sexton and Robert Lowell and labeled all of them "confessional poets," as a way of dealing with the new and often shockingly personal subject matter all three poets wrote about.[13] What I've come to call the misogynist response in early Plath criticism is exemplified by Philip Hosbaum and Edward Butscher. Hosbaum, in "The Temptation of Giant Despair," a review of *The Savage God*, dismisses the female world view Plath presents in her poetry and indeed, that of all the "ladies of the confessional school," as he calls them, while carefully removing the label of "confessional poet" from Robert Lowell, who in *Life Studies* and *For the Union Dead* had used a similar autobiographical mode.[14] Edward Butscher's 1975 book, *Sylvia Plath: Method and Madness*, takes a biographical/psychological approach; while it does offer some interesting material about Plath's life which had not been previously available, it makes of Plath a "bitch goddess" (Butscher's term), mythologizing her as Lowell had done, but less sympathetically.[15] An early example of feminist criticism, that is, a criticism that takes Plath's gender as significant in explaining the relation between her life and her writing, is Harriet Rosenstein's unsympathetic article in *Ms.* on *The Bell Jar*, where she says of the novel's protagonist, Esther Greenwood, that she "looks everywhere for female models and finds none, less the result of an impoverished culture than of her own impoverished ego";[16] a more balanced and biographical early feminist approach to Plath is Sandra Gilbert's article in *Shakespeare's Sisters*, "A Fine, White Flying Myth: The Life/Work of Sylvia Plath."[17]

A new era of Plath criticism opened with Judith Kroll's *Chapters in a Mythology* (1976), which began the important task of reading Sylvia Plath's poems rather than her life. Rather than making Plath herself into a myth, Kroll traced the ways in which Plath had used mythology, often quite consciously.[18] Margaret Uroff's book on Sylvia Plath and Ted Hughes was a much needed account of the way these two major twentieth-century poets influenced each other in a close working relationship probably only rivaled by Robert and Elizabeth Barrett Browning almost a century earlier.[19] Jon Rosenblatt's *Sylvia Plath: The Poetry of Initiation* was the first general, as opposed to specialized, study of the poems that treated

Plath primarily as a poet of major stature rather than as a writer who had committed suicide and written about her intention to do so.[20] Rosenblatt does, however, downplay the significance both of Plath's gender and of her social and historical context.

Changes in Plath criticism have been affected to some extent by the resource material available in print. As regards the poetry, *The Colossus* is unique in being the only collection of her work Plath herself arranged. The subsequent collections of poetry, *Ariel*, *Crossing the Water*, and *Winter Trees*, were selected and arranged by Ted Hughes. Hughes's suggestion that the poems of *Crossing the Water* were transitional provoked Marjorie Perloff's rebuttal that in fact they weren't so neatly transitional.[21] *Winter Trees* was even more shapeless as a collection, though, perhaps because it included the first publication of Plath's verse play, *Three Women*. Charles Newman's early anthology, *The Art of Sylvia Plath*, had included a number of biographical resources as well as articles on the work.[22] Other resource material began appearing in print in 1975 with the publication, heavily edited, of Plath's letters to her mother, *Letters Home*. A collection of Plath's short stories, titled after the most interesting of them, *Johnny Panic and the Bible of Dreams*, appeared in 1977. *The Collected Poems*, finally published in 1981 and arranged chronologically, included some 50 of the juvenilia (unfortunately, many not dated) and a table of contents of Plath's own version of *Ariel*. Hughes, in the introduction to *The Collected Poems*, suggests three phases in Plath's work: the juvenilia up to the end of 1955, the poems of the *Colossus* period, early 1956 to late 1960, and the late poems, from September 1960 to her death in early 1963.[23] In 1982 appeared the most interesting resource to date, Plath's *Journals*, important not only for Plath scholars and readers but a major event in the genre of women's autobiographical writing. Drawing from the journals and the letters and basing her study of Plath's poems and novel on the feminist theory of Simone de Beauvoir, Adrienne Rich, and Nancy Chodorow, Lynda K. Bundtzen, in *Plath's Incarnations: Woman and the Creative Process*, produced the first book-length feminist study of Sylvia Plath's work.[24]

The present study traces, through the internal dialectics that structure the poems, the evolution of Plath's imagery and personae from *The Colossus* through *Ariel*; it looks at the way the poems embody the tension between images of self and images of world, or context within which the self exists, and it looks at the struggles within the poems to achieve transformation of self and of self in relation to world. A major American poet writing in a period of literary transition from modernism to postmodernism, Sylvia Plath determinedly and fiercely wrote of and out of female experience and in the context of the time and place that shaped her—the mid 1950s to the early 1960s, in a post–World War II and prefeminist United States. Sylvia Plath is in many ways transitional. She wrote in a period of retreat in American life and art from the explicitly political, in a period of postwar prosperity and political passivity accompanied by a resurgence of American individualism and the success ethic; a time of *kinder* and *kuche* if not necessarily *kirche* for American women, a time when if a woman expected to have a career she had better plan to be a successful wife and mother as well. Plath's life exemplifies the tension and stresses of the success ethic and the role expectation conflict faced by any woman who had creative talent and a calling ("the blood jet is poetry, / There is no stopping it" ["Kindness", 1963]) and who also wanted to fulfill the conventional roles expected of women. Plath says over and over in her journals and letters that she had the energy and strength to do it all but the stress must have been tremendous. Had she been born ten years later, she might not have felt the same kind of pressures; her choices, her solutions, her poetry might have been different. Within the fifteen years after Plath's death, the United States moved into a period of social protest and increasing political consciousness, some, though not all of it, concentrated around the Civil Rights movement, the anti–Vietnam War movement, and the women's movement. In response, American poetry became more explicitly political on the one hand and more concerned with narrating the poet's personal engagement with a real world. It became less ironic and detached, more engaged, committed, and subjective; it became a poetry of involvement as well as a poetry of experience. The changes in American consciousness that would make possible Denise Levertov's anti-war poems in the late 1960s and Adrienne Rich's feminist poems by the early 1970s were not available to Plath in the late 1950s and early 1960s.

Plath does indicate, in two separate 1962 comments about her own work, her concern about connecting personal experience with political commitment or at the least with putting personal experience into a political context. Employing again the mirror image, she said in a BBC interview:

I think that personal experience is very important, but certainly it shouldn't be a kind of shut-box and mirror-looking, narcissistic experience. I believe it should be relevant, and relevant to the larger things, the bigger things, such as Hiroshima and Dachau.[25]

"Context," a 1962 essay, illustrates Plath's awareness of the dangers of nuclear war and monopoly capitalism; it also demonstrates that, as an artist writing about her own work, Plath had not yet resolved the current separation between personal and political or seen her poetry as a direct and conscious way of connecting the two or mediating between them.

The issues of our time which preoccupy me at the moment are the incalculable genetic effects of fallout and a documentary article on the terrifying, mad, omnipotent marriage of big business and the military in America—"Juggernaut, the Warfare State," by Fred J. Cook in a recent *Nation*. Does this influence the kind of poetry I write? Yes, but in a sidelong fashion. I am not gifted with the tongue of Jeremiah, though I may be sleepless enough before my vision of the apocalypse. My poems do not turn out to be about Hiroshima, but about a child forming itself finger by finger in the dark. They are not about the terrors of mass extinction, but about the bleakness of the moon over a yew in a neighboring graveyard. Not about the testaments of tortured Algerians, but about the night thoughts of a tired surgeon.

In a sense these poems are deflections. I do not think they are an escape. For me, the real issues of our time are the issues of every time—the hurt and wonder of loving; making in all its forms, children, loaves of bread, paintings, buildings; and the conservation of all people in all places, the jeopardizing of which no abstract doubletalk of "peace" or "implacable foes" can excuse.

I do not think a "headline poetry" would interest more people any more profoundly than the headlines. And unless the up-to-the-minute poem grows out of something closer to the bone than a general, shifting philanthropy and is, indeed, that unicorn thing—a real poem—it is in danger of being screwed up as rapidly as the news sheet itself.[26]

Similarly, Denise Levertov wrote in 1959:

I do not believe that a violent imitation of the horrors of our times is the concern of poetry. . . . I long for poems of an inner harmony in utter contrast to the chaos in which they exist. Insofar as poetry has a social function it is to awaken sleepers by other means than shock.[27]

In the light of Levertov's own later political poetry, she felt that she needed to add a postscript to this statement in 1973, explaining that she had not been talking about the content of poetry, but about form. Nevertheless, I think it was a particular poetic and political climate that produced both the original statements by Plath and Levertov and the postscript by Levertov. Though Plath denies that her poems are explicitly political, what she does do, especially in her late poems, is to use the brutality of war and the alienation of bureaucracy as metaphors for the relation between self and world. And she offers a series of personae who vibrate with barely suppressed and explosive anger at their containment. She explores the relations and the tension between self and world, especially a female self and a mid-twentieth century American world. Her poems are perhaps the most brilliant evocation of this time and place we have as they are experienced by a creative, determined, and angry woman, and I think it is to that locus of preexplosive power in Plath's work that my students were responding.

This book is a developmental study of the imagery of Sylvia Plath's poetry. Chapter Two, on poems of *The Colossus*, discusses the social implications of mythic imagery in Plath's early poetry. Chapter Three looks at the poems of the middle period and focuses on the relationship between language, imagery, and sexual/social context and on the trapped situation of a woman poet trying to define herself through a medium whose assumptions are inimical to that act of self definition. Chapter Four explores, through Plath's verse play *Three Women*, the connections between aesthetic and biological creativity in a bureaucratic, depersonalized world. Chapter Five, on the *Ariel* poems, is centered on the internalized conflict of self and society within the poet; it deals with Sylvia Plath's sense of paralysis and discusses Plath's various attempts, metaphorically and within the poems, to narrate the possibilities for a transformed self reborn into a transformed world.

NOTES

1. Sylvia Plath, "The Magic Mirror," from the Sylvia Plath manuscript collection, The Lilly Library, Indiana University, p. 1.

2. Ibid., p. 2.

3. Ibid., p. 7.

4. Ibid., pp. 59–60.

5. Virginia Woolf, *A Room of One's Own* (New York: Harcourt, Brace & World, 1929), p. 101.

6. Cora Kaplan, "Language and Gender," in *Papers on Patriarchy* (London: Women's Publishing Collective, 1976), p. 29. Quoted in Dale Spender, *Man-Made Language* (London: Routledge & Kegan Paul, 1980), p. 192.

7. Cheryl Walker, *The Nightingale's Burden: Women Poets and American Culture Before 1900* (Bloomington: Indiana University Press, 1982), p. 38.

8. Ibid., pp. 9–10.

9. Sylvia Plath, *The Journals of Sylvia Plath* (New York: Dial Press, 1982), pp. 211–12.

10. Robert Lowell, "Foreword" in Sylvia Plath, *Ariel* (New York: Harper & Row, 1965), p. vii.

11. A. Alvarez, *The Savage God: A Study of Suicide* (Middlesex, England: Penguin, 1974), pp. 19–60.

12. Robin Morgan, "Arraignment" in *Monster* (New York: Vintage, 1972), pp. 76–78.

13. M. L. Rosenthal, *The New Poets* (New York: Oxford University Press, 1967), pp. 79–89.

14. Philip Hosbaum, "The Temptation of Giant Despair" in *Hudson Review* 25 (Winter 1972–73): 607.

15. Edward Butscher, *Sylvia Plath: Method and Madness* (New York: Seabury Press, 1976).

16. Harriet Rosenstein, "Reconsidering Sylvia Plath" *Ms. Magazine*, September 1972, p. 48.

17. Sandra M. Gilbert, "A Fine White Flying Myth: The Life/Work of Sylvia Plath" in *Shakespeare's Sisters: Feminist Essays on Women Poets*, ed. Sandra M. Gilbert and Susan Gubar (Bloomington: Indiana University Press, 1979), pp. 245–60.

18. Judith Kroll, *Chapters in a Mythology: The Poetry of Sylvia Plath* (New York: Harper & Row, 1976).

19. Margaret Dickie Uroff, *Sylvia Plath and Ted Hughes* (Urbana: University of Illinois Press, 1979).

20. Jon Rosenblatt, *Sylvia Plath: The Poetry of Initiation* (Chapel Hill: The University of North Carolina Press, 1979).

21. Marjorie Perloff, "On the Road to Ariel: The 'Transitional' Poetry of Sylvia Plath" in *Sylvia Plath: The Woman and the Work*, Edward Butscher, ed. (New York: Dodd, Mead, 1977), pp. 125–42.

22. Charles Newman, ed., *The Art of Sylvia Plath* (Bloomington: Indiana University Press, 1970).

23. Ted Hughes, "Introduction" in *Sylvia Plath: The Collected Poems*, Ted Hughes, ed. (New York: Harper & Row, 1981), pp. 15–17.

24. Lynda K. Bundtzen, *Plath's Incarnations: Woman and the Creative Process* (Ann Arbor: University of Michigan Press, 1983).

25. Peter Orr, *The Poet Speaks* (New York: Barnes and Noble, 1966), pp. 169–70.

26. Sylvia Plath, *Johnny Panic and the Bible of Dreams: Short Stories, Prose, and Diary Excerpts* (New York: Harper & Row, 1979), pp. 64–65.

27. Denise Levertov, "A Testament and a Postscript, 1959–1973" in *The Poet in the World* (New York: New Directions, 1973), pp. 3–6.

❧ 2 ❧

The Colossus: In Search of a Self

The tradition of the dead generations weighs
like a nightmare on the brain of the living.

—Karl Marx[1]

They had no tradition behind them, or one so
short and partial that it was of little help.

—Virginia Woolf[2]

The landscapes of Sylvia Plath's poems, her images of the world—
that large inclusive other with which she finally declines to interact—gradually develop from natural and supernatural to historical
and social. The personae of her poems reflect a corresponding
change. While in the later poems they are increasingly seen as not
separate from the world but of it and unable to move in relation
to it, in *The Colossus* she is still imagining forays across the boundary
lines between self and world. In these early poems there is a possibility of choice and movement which gradually rigidifies in her
later work as her images of the world become inclusive of her
images of self. As her landscapes change, as the poems themselves
narrate the poet entering history, her possibilities for transformation decrease though her desire for transformation does not.

The Colossus presents a world in which characters from fairy tale and myth peer through the England and New England land-scapes of stone and sea which form the surface setting of many of the poems. The geography of Sylvia Plath's imaged world and her relationship to it in her first volume of poems is characterized by fluid boundaries. With their mythic and fairy tale atmosphere projected onto nature, the poems in *The Colossus* form a locus for actual or potential transformations. From the donning of the per-sona of a community of mushrooms or frogs to the yearning to join her sisters the Lorelei, the poet of *The Colossus* poems lives in a twilight world between reality and myth and between her own imaged self and the rest of her imaged world. The speaking sensibility of those early poems is, for the most part, alone in a world of natural images and dusty museum pieces from the past, of which the gigantic and fragmented statue of her father in the title poem is the most problematic. Because the boundaries of this world are fluid, it is a realm of potentiality. One could become anything. The speaking sensibility of these poems wanders through familiar scenes, but what she sees, sometimes lurking behind and sometimes superimposed on this natural setting—marble women beckoning to her from under the surface of a river, her father's face in the sea, attenuated spindly shapes of people pressing through the walls of her room—are weird figures that represent possibility or constraint. The landscape of *The Colossus* poems is shifting and fluid; so is the identity of the speaker, who attempts various trans-formations—into a mushroom, a mole, a stone. Both the self-image of the speaker of the poems and the world with which she interacts are, in *The Colossus*, in flux. Images of stone and sea, recurrent in *The Colossus*, are intertwined with the supernatural. Both represent the alienness of nature, the world which exists out-side the poet. The speaker of the poems has a complex relation-ship to a nature imaged as stone and sea: She is both repelled by it and attracted to it. Nature is seen as impervious to the self; the human individual finds it incomprehensible and dangerous in the sense that one can break oneself on it and leave no trace. Also nature is seen as hostile to the self not so much in actual malevo-lence but in its very alienness; here it is not repellent but yielding, and the self is in danger of dissolving into what surrounds her.

The subject of *The Colossus* poems is the boundary between self and other; Plath's concern in these early poems is with where the boundary lines are, of what they consist, whether and how they can be passed, and whether the traveler can get back. Like the composite hero of Joseph Campbell's monomyth, Sylvia Plath in her early poems charts a voyage out into the unknown and back again; she consciously utilizes structures of myth and fairy tale to point a contrast between a childhood memory of potentiality and a recognition of the constraints and limits of the world she in fact inhabits.

"Hardcastle Crags," written while Plath was living in England in 1956–57, is a microcosm of this movement out and back again. The poem is built around a recurrent and finally overwhelming image of stone. The narrative surface of the poem tells simply how one night a woman leaves a town, walks out in the surrounding countryside, and finally retreats in fear back into the town. The poem is beautifully structured upon two contrasts, and transcends them. The woman's increase in knowledge about the real nature of the world she lives in and her position in it parallel the stages of her journey out into the night and back. Told in the third person, "Hardcastle Crags" forces the reader's progressive discoveries about the nature of the poem's imaged world to parallel those of the woman adventurer.

The poem seems at first to set up a contrast and an opposition between the artificiality of the town and the naturalness of the world outside the town.

> Flintlike, her feet struck
> Such a racket of echoes from the steely street,
> Tacking in moon-blued crooks from the black
> Stone-built town, that she heard the quick air ignite
> Its tinder and shake
>
> A firework of echoes from wall
> To wall of the dark, dwarfed cottages.
> But the echoes died at her back as the walls
> Gave way to fields and the incessant seethe of grasses
> Riding in the full
>
> Of the moon, manes to the wind,
> Tireless, tied, as a moon-bound sea
> Moves on its root.

The town is described in images of stone and steel, alien and far removed from the sensual possibilities of life. The people who live in this town have taken on the characteristics of their surroundings. The woman is part of her environment; her feet are "flint-like" and strike echoes against the stone and steel. In fact, this is the only sound within the city: People and their artifacts echoing each other in an endless clamour.

The woman in "Hardcastle Crags" leaves the town, hoping to find in the night and the natural world outside something to correspond to her own potential sensuality and silence. At first there does seem to be a contrast between the echoing racket of the static town and the silent and moving world outside: "The walls / Gave way to fields and the incessant seethe of grasses." But the grasses are not free; they are "tied." The possibility of free movement, of a place where one can develop and change rather than merely strike echoes, fades as she walks further into this alien land where the mist turns to no "family-featured ghost."

Instead of finding an alternative to the static stone of the town, she finds herself confronting something even more alien. If she left the town in rejection of one mode of life or one image of herself in relation to her world, and her flight into the fields is an attempt at a redefinition or rebirth of her self, then it fails, partly because she is made of the stuff of the town.

> All the night gave her, in return
> For the paltry gift of her bulk and the beat
> Of her heart, was the humped indifferent iron
> Of its hills, and its pastures bordered by black stone set
> On black stone.

All she sees in the natural world which should have life and movement and with which she could identify has been turned to stone. All untied organic life (animals, birds) has been petrified, immobilized. All that moves freely is "the long wind, paring her person down / To a pinch of flame." Everything else she perceives in the natural world is stone; it is so alien that it is finally primeval slag, a prehuman world "unaltered by eyes." She is in mortal danger there and survives only by turning, finally, back to the town.

In addition to the contrast between the town and the world

outside the town which has proved false and static, there is an apparent contrast in the poem between the warmth and freedom of the woman's movement and the two realms of stone which form the poles of her world. However, "flintlike," the woman does initially partake of the stonelike quality of the town; and in the last stanza of the poem, she also is potentially part of the stoniness that the world outside has been transformed into:

> . . . but before the weight
> Of stones and hills of stones could break
> Her down to mere quartz grit in that stony light
> She turned back.

She too is a stone, then, but a less impervious stone, a fractured stone, one that can be broken up: flint in contrast to the steel of the town, quartz in contrast to the granite of the natural world outside the town. Both the human and the nonhuman world have become objectified and the woman herself becomes an object, petrified, reified, and dehumanized. In "Hardcastle Crags" the difference between the self and the world that surrounds it is in degree of imperviousness. The self comes up against something more complete, finished, opaque, strong, less able to be broken down into fragments than she is. Finally, the world of the town is less frightening than the world outside; in the town she can at least "strike echoes" rather than be broken down to "mere quartz grit."

The task the woman of "Hardcastle Crags" had set herself was to bring life and consciousness to a stone-frozen static world and perhaps to find her own identity through the quest. The intention of her adventure is not unlike what Joseph Campbell describes, in *Hero with a Thousand Faces*, as the timeless and primal adventure of the hero, who finds that either he or the world in which he lives

suffers from a symbolical deficiency. In fairy tales this may be as slight as the lack of a certain golden ring, whereas in apocalyptic vision the physical and spiritual life of the whole earth can be represented as fallen, or on the point of falling, into ruin.[3]

The hero leaves a world which is, like the world of the town in "Hardcastle Crags," like the post-war, post-atomic bomb world of both Joseph Campbell and Sylvia Plath, in some way deficient or diminished. He goes out into the unknown and there wins and brings back across the boundaries some power which will regenerate his own life, his society, or both. The hero's journey is actually through an inner landscape, however. What he gains is not something new but an increased knowledge of what he already possessed. "The godly powers sought and dangerously won," writes Campbell, "are revealed to have been within the heart of the hero all the time. He is 'the king's son' who has come to know who he is and therewith has entered into the exercise of his proper power—'God's son,' who has learned to know how much that title means."[4] Campbell's monomyth is based on patriarchal myths which describe an individual hero who becomes an effectual shaper of history through his discovery that he is part of a tradition and that there is a place for him in an already existing pattern. But what if the journey that you have embarked on reveals to you that you are not "the king's son" or "God's son"? What if, instead of discovering your power, you discover that you are powerless? What if, instead of discovering a tradition you are legitimate heir to, you find that you are dispossessed and will have to steal it or do without? For a woman to accept this mythic pattern whole and then attempt to apply it to her own life is to court disappointment and defeat. The colossus that the speaker of Sylvia Plath's early poems confronts (in the title poem of this first volume) is a gigantic male statue which fills the entire field of her vision and of which she says, "I shall never get you put together entirely."

In *The Colossus* Sylvia Plath focuses on the boundaries between herself and her world to test the limits of action both imaginative and real. On the one hand, the speaker of these poems yearns for the Apollonian choice of rationality and order, which implies separation between self and world and control of world by self. On the other hand, the poems express a Dionysian desire to transcend the boundaries of self and to merge with a larger other, to undergo transformation and in the process to become wordless. Many of the poems in *The Colossus* are about a literal transformation into a nonhuman persona; and "metamorphosis into an object in the world of nature," suggests Northrop Frye, "represents the falling silent of the world in its human or rational phase."[5] The Apollonian/Dionysian tension within the imaged self of Plath's poems is synonymous with another choice, between stasis and movement. In so far as movement implies incompletion and therefore imperfection, it is related to the uncategorized and the Dionysian, while stasis suggests completion and therefore perfection, that which is grasped and categorized, and is related to the Apollonian. We go to Apollo to hear a prophecy, to get advice, to fix the unknown in words; we go to Dionysus to join in the dance. The tension between Apollo and Dionysus in these early poems places the rational, man-made, ordered, and comprehensible against the arational, sensual, nonhuman, disordered, passionate, transcendent, and incomprehensible—at least by the usual human approaches to understanding phenomena. And of course the means by which one's world is controlled, especially and self-consciously so if one is a poet, is through words. The speaker of these poems is attracted to and repelled by both these choices, and the tension is worked out in subjects both light and profound.

In "Spinster" (1956), a wryly humorous poem, a girl becomes aware of an assault upon her senses during a springtime walk. The season is described in Apollonian negatives, as "irregular," unbalanced, uneven. "She judged petals in disarray, / The whole season, sloven." Set against spring is winter, "scrupulously austere in its order / Of black and white." Though tempted by the sensuality of the season, the speaker of the poem finally chooses disengagement, retreat to a self-created world whose every aspect she controls. "Let idiots / Reel giddy in bedlam spring: / She withdrew neatly." The final image of "Spinster" ("And round her house she set / Such a barricade of barb and check") is of a closed-off life, a person ringed with barbed wire, enclosed within defined boundaries, and possessed of a control of her environment such that nothing will ever threaten her, or pleasantly surprise her. Order is set against chaos, winter against spring, austerity against burgeoning, balance against tumult, the "heart's frosty discipline" against the possibility of love.

This choice, like that of the student who gives her child away in *Three Women*, is not one Plath herself finally feels drawn to, even though she believes that the sterility of this choice, its lack of commitment, is appropriate to the age she lives in. She extends the girl's choice to a social level in "The Times Are Tidy" (1958): "Unlucky the hero born / In this province of the stuck record," she writes. This is a world where "There's no career in the venture / Of riding against the lizard," and "The last crone got burnt up / More than eight decades back"—"But the children are better for it." Plath mourns this abdication to the realistic, which in her later poems becomes even more specifically the portrait of a bureaucratic, reified society, in much the same way that Yeats did in his 1914 volume, *Responsibilities*. The "dragon-guarded land" of Yeats's "The Realists" is not unlike Plath's lost world in "The Times are Tidy." However, Yeats's closing lines, evoking "a hope to live / That had gone / With the dragons,"[6] are wistful where Plath's, "But the children are better for it" is bitterly ironic. Yeats and Plath, each in their early poetry, set up a contrast between their present age—mercenary, bureaucratic, and depersonalized, an age where the heroic is no longer possible—and another time imaged through legend, myth, and fairy tale, where it seemed possible to fulfill some kind of heroic and individual potential. Both initially looked for a mythic coherence and structure for their poetry. Yeats saw what he considered the stable values of an aristocratic and folk way of life, based on feudalism, replaced by the shifting and superficial values of the marketplace. The modern American poet, including Plath, saw the loss of the kind of potentiality articulated in the nineteenth century by Whitman. Like Yeats in his middle period, Sylvia Plath moves from a search for herself in myth, legend, and fairy tale to find a poetic structure in historical events. And, as Carolyn Heilbrun points out, Emily Dickinson's words, "I'm nobody," are a more significant legacy for twentieth-century women writers than Whitman's 'I celebrate myself and sing myself.'[7]

In *The Colossus*, Plath's attempt to conjoin two initially separate images, herself and a problematic world, takes the form of attempted transformations of self. The speaking sensibility of the poems tries to undergo a metamorphosis into the world of nature in two ways: into animate nature, as in "Blue Moles" (1959), "Frog Autumn" (1958), "Flute Notes from a Reedy Pond" (1959), and "Mushrooms" (1959), or into inanimate nature, in "The Lorelei" (1958), "Full Fathom Five" (1958), and "Suicide Off Egg Rock" (1959). "The Stones" (1959) is Plath's final and most significant attempt at transformation in *The Colossus*, where she attempts to become what she fled from in "Hardcastle Crags."

While Ted Hughes in his poetry chose to identify with the powerful and predatory aspects of nature, e.g., the pike, the crow, the wolf—Sylvia Plath most often takes on nonhuman personae which are small, weak and unobtrusive. And while Hughes' animal personae are solitary and individual, Plath, in her poems of identification with what we think of as nature's victimized or unnoticed, often does not focus on an individual but speaks communally as "we." "Blue Moles," "Mushrooms," and "Flute Notes from a Reedy Pond" (part 5 of "Poem for a Birthday") were written in the fall of 1959 at Yaddo, "Frog Autumn" during 1957–58 while Plath was teaching at Smith College. In "Blue Moles" we watch the metamorphosis of the speaker take place. She comments in her own person in Part One on two dead moles, "shapeless as flung gloves," which she has seen by the side of the road; in Part Two, she transforms herself into a mole. Both the poem and the transformation seem done as an exercise. Ted Hughes says of "Mushrooms," another poem from this group, that it "developed from an invocation" and it seems that this three-month period at Yaddo was a time of conscious experimentation with voice for Plath. Of her work during this period, Hughes writes:

The sudden enrichment of the texture of her verse, and the nimble shifting of focus, were something new and surprised her. At this time, she was concentratedly trying to break down the tyranny, the fixed focus and public persona which descriptive or discoursive poems take as a norm.[8]

"Frog Autumn," a lament by the amphibious inhabitants of a pond for the end of summer, speaks of decay, the withering of all life, hunger—"our folk thin / Lamentably"—and a growing somnolence. "Flute Notes from a Reedy Pond" treats the same situation, but the tone has changed. While "Frog Autumn" was a lament which came from ignorance of one's own relation to the larger scheme of things, "Flute Notes from A Reedy Pond" finds a comfort in the "soft caul of forgetfulness." A drift into the passivity of hibernation is seen positively in this poem. The inhabitants of the pond, aware that they are part of the cycle of nature, are also aware that the end of one cycle has come. They are tired and have no desire to remain conscious through the winter, have no desire even for it to remain summer. Unlike the frogs in the earlier poem, they welcome an end of activity. And besides, "this is not death, it is something safer." The reference in the last stanza to the crucifixion both reemphasizes their victimization and suggests that the frogs are merely passing into an oblivion which precedes a rebirth.

"Mushrooms," written at about the same time as "Flute Notes from a Reedy Pond," seems at first the most positive statement of self, a waking up rather than a going to sleep. Spoken by a communal persona, it is in one sense about creativity, revolution, and the meek inheriting the earth. The mushrooms are described as small, discreet, soft, quiet, bland-mannered; as individuals, unnoticeable, as a group, indomitable.

> Overnight, very
> Whitely, discreetly
> Very quietly
>
> Our toes, our noses
> Take hold on the loam,
> Acquire the air.

The mood of the poem is playful and humorous, the lines short, the breath units quick, the general impression one of little bursts of growth. In one sense, this is a poem of fulfillment and potency. The very unobtrusiveness of the mushrooms, the very fact that they ask for little and appear to constitute a danger to no one, makes for their success.

> We are shelves, we are
> Tables, we are meek,
> We are edible,
>
> Nudgers and shovers
> In spite of ourselves.
> Our kind multiplies:
>
> We shall by morning
> Inherit the earth.
> Our foot's in the door.

The poem, however, makes one uneasy; perhaps because, like early Afro-American spirituals, "Mushrooms" is a fantasy of power and

powerlessness in which the elements of resentment and acquies-
ence, anger and Christian humility, are curiously mixed. The featureless "heads" of the mushrooms which push out from the earth
are reminiscent of the studies of black and working class children
which found them drawing figures of people with no hands. Their
blankness is not unlike the stone imagery which characterizes Plath's
poems from this period. Nor are they unlike the featureless darning-egg heads of the figures she calls in this volume her disquieting muses, which turn in *Ariel* into an image of the barren moon.
All four of these images are characterized by a lack of senses: no
eyes and ears with which to perceive, no mouth with which to
speak. And in addition to being sense-less, mushrooms are edible.

Even in the poems which make up *The Colossus*, then, the
imaginative forays across the boundary lines are usually inter-
rupted, the transformations only partial. The apparent innocence
of transforming oneself into a community of frogs or mushrooms
is even more problematic in those poems where the speaker tries
to merge with inanimate nature. That the inanimate world outside
the self is alien to the self and hostile in its alienness, that the self
in seeking out this world is in danger of dissolving into it or being
engulfed by it, is a major theme in Plath's poetry. To face what
is outside the self is to confront her own extinction, and the possibility both draws and repels her. "Suicide Off Egg Rock" (1959)
records the case of one who, unlike the woman in "Hardcastle
Crags" and unlike Esther Greenwood in *The Bell Jar*, does not
turn back.[9]

As in "Blue Moles," Plath's method in "Suicide Off Egg Rock"
is to move from outside to inside. The first stanza records the
character's perceptions of the scene around him, the second stanza
moves to his perception of himself and thence to action. The world
he is in, though near the sea, is dominated by people and their
artifacts and adjutants, from the "hotdogs split and drizzled / On
the public grills" to the factories to the squealing children and
mongrel dog. The sounds and images are ugly and disjunctive. It
is a "landscape / Of imperfections," which has set itself apart from
nature or rather superimposed itself on nature, and the natural
world condemns it. "Sun struck the water like a damnation." This
is an oppressive scene to the speaker of the poem, but nonetheless
one he knows he is part of. The second stanza shows him taking

on the characteristics of this "landscape / Of imperfections his bowels were part of—." He too becomes a "machine to breathe and beat forever." The vision he has had in stanza one is so bleak, so depressing, that his reaction is to switch off, to become "stone-deaf, blindfold." Faced with a world gone meaningless, he himself becomes meaningless except for the possibility of oblivion which death can provide. Finally, the only image which pierces his self-imposed blindness is the sea and Egg Rock; the only sensuous image in the poem is the final description of the sea which holds out death: "He heard when he walked into the water / The forgetful surf creaming on those ledges."

"Lorelei" opens with a line which seems to contradict the conclusion of "Suicide Off Egg Rock." The speaker of the poem says: "It is no night to drown in." But it is a cry which protests too much, for she is in fact attracted by the oblivion, peace, and static perfection which the dark river promises. This call is metaphorized as the Lorelei, folk-tale figures of women whom Plath sees as sisters. From Plath's journal for July 4, 1958:

Last night Ted and I did PAN [ouija board] for the first time in America. . . . Kolossus is Pan's "family god." . . . Pan said I should write on the poem subject 'Lorelei' because they are my "own kin." So today for fun I did so, remembering the plaintive German song Mother used to play and sing to us beginning "Ich weiss nicht was solles bedeuten. . . . " The subject appealed to me doubly (or triply): The German legend of the Rhine sirens, the sea-childhood symbol, and the death-wish involved in the song's beauty.[10]

With their "hair heavier / Than sculpted marble," the Lorelei have a created, finished, and larger-than-life perfection which the speaker of the poem envies. They also represent the dark Dionysian forces which are opposed to and exist "beyond the mundane order." The fascination of this dark other world is, in the end, overwhelming and the speaking sensibility of the poem ends with a plea to join them: "Stone, stone, ferry me down there."

"Full Fathom Five" was written about the same time as "Lorelei" and the yearning for another world, beyond the ordered rational human world, where peace and stillness reign, also characterizes this poem. The river before was identified with her "sisters."

Here the image of her father (who died when she was eight) is superimposed on the sea, and a return to the sea becomes a reunion with her dead father. Her father is often connected with the sea, certainly in "The Colossus" and "Daddy" and also in "All the Dead Dears": "Where the daft father went down / With orange duck-feet winnowing his hair—." In "Full Fathom Five" the face of the sea itself is the face of an old white-haired man who in the final stanza she calls father. As in "The Colossus" he is an overwhelming figure: "Miles long / Extend the radial sheaves / Of your spread hair." Not only mysterious, appearing and disappearing, he is also dangerous, as an iceberg, which can wreck a ship not because of what is seen but what is unseen: "All obscurity / Starts with a danger: / Your dangers are many." He will wear away the land and sky on which she leans, given enough time. In spite of the obvious danger of merging with what is so alien, she longs for a reunion which would also be death. "I walk dry on your kingdom's border / Exiled to no good. / Your shelled bed I remember." What she wants is a transformation which would make reunion possible. Already half there, she is not happy where she now is; the present is also death. "Father, this thick air is murderous. / I would breathe water." Kate Chopin's Edna Pontillier thinks as she walks into the ocean to drown at the end of *The Awakening* (1899): "The voice of the sea is seductive . . . The touch of the sea is sensuous, enfolding the body in its soft, close embrace."[11] That a number of twentieth century women writers have had their characters choose, seriously consider, or vehemently reject suicide—or madness, which could perhaps be seen as a reluctance to confront suicide as one of a list of dwindling possibilities—indicates the extent to which women writers from Chopin to Plath have felt both powerless and repressed.

Testifying both to this sense of powerlessness and to the necessity for still making choices, even though the range of choice is severely limited, are the fairy-tale characters which Plath uses throughout her poetry. From the reference to the neglected and malevolent bad fairy of "Sleeping Beauty" in "The Disquieting Muses" to the Lorelei and the nursery rhyme rhythms of "The Bull of Bendylaw" and "Daddy," the elemental passion and the frightening or attractive figures of a childhood world of fantasy move, often with terrifying immediacy, through the world of her poems. Two fairy-tale characters which Plath uses in presenting her own self-image in *The Colossus* are particularly suggestive: Sleeping Beauty and the Little Mermaid.

In "Sleeping Beauty" the princess pricks her finger on a spindle in early adolescence, symbolizing the onset of menstruation.[12] She falls asleep and the rest of her world falls asleep with her until the appointed hundred years is up and a prince rides in to rescue her. In a patriarchal society that sees women as property, this is a neat and efficient means of storage of female adolescents. The daughter sleeps in a room at the top of an isolated tower until she can be passed on undamaged to a new owner in marriage. In the sense that, when she becomes unconscious, the rest of her immediate world is suspended until she awakes, the point of view in "Sleeping Beauty" is the princess's. This hundred-year sleep suggests her own unconscious acceptance of social values. They are imposed upon her, and she internalizes them. Throughout the tale, the princess has no choice. Her life is mapped out for her while she is still in the cradle by thirteen older women (in Plath's poem "The Disquieting Muses," three of them nod about her bed); in one variant of the tale these are fairies, in another wise women. The princess also has no choice over the means and time of her awakening and, since the prince who wakes her is the only one she's ever seen, much less kissed, she has not much information on which to base choices about the rest of her life either.

What differentiates the unnamed princess of Hans Christian Anderson's "The Little Mermaid" from the princess of "Sleeping Beauty" is her degree of consciousness and her control over her own destiny.[13] The youngest of six princesses, she is from the beginning more thoughtful and more interested in the world above the sea than any of her five sisters. When she is fifteen, she sees and falls in love with a handsome prince and, moreover, saves him from drowning, establishing her own capacity for action. She asks the sea witch to transform her into a human so she can capture the prince's love. There is more at stake here than just a husband, however, for the only way a mermaid (or merman), according to Anderson, can gain an immortal soul is through the love of a human being. The sea witch consents to mix a potion which will transform the mermaid into a human, but only under two conditions. The first is that the transformation itself will be painful, like a sword going through her body, and, afterward, every time her foot touches the ground it will feel like she has walked on sharp knives. The second condition is that her tongue will be cut out. The transformation that the little mermaid chooses involves self-sacrifice. She must give up her ability to move without pain and she must give up her ability to speak and to sing in order to try for the prince's love and for a soul. But in contrast to Sleeping Beauty, who waits unconscious until her prince finds her, and in contrast even to Cinderella (the third prototypical image of the young woman in fairy-tale) who teases her prince so that he will run after her and who would still be sitting in the ashes if her fairy godmother had not miraculously appeared, the little mermaid, at every point in her adventure, chooses her own destiny. In all three tales, the movement of the narrative is toward marriage; only in "The Little Mermaid" is marriage not an end in itself, but a means.

It is not hard to see how this childhood story would have captured Sylvia Plath's imagination such that she might see herself as the woman caught between land and sea, who has bartered her mermaid's fins for feet on which she will forever walk as though on sharp knives, who sits at night on the shore forever gazing out on the sea she has renounced and can no longer live in. Plath's journal (April 22, 1958):

Yesterday was wiped out by the cramps and drug-stitched stupor of my first day of the curse, as it is so aptly called. Do animals in heat bleed, feel pain? Or is it that sedentary bluestockinged ladies have come so far from the beast-state that they must pay by hurt, as the little mermaid had to pay when she traded her fishtail for a girl's white legs?[14]

Part of the poignancy of Sylvia Plath's early poems comes from this sense of being caught between two worlds, a part of both and therefore wholly of neither.

The story elements of "The Little Mermaid" continue to turn up, though in more disguised and distorted forms, in *Ariel*. "Fever 103°" has the speaker of the poem rising to become a kind of air spirit, as the little mermaid does at the end of that story, but by this time Plath's tone is mocking. In "Daddy," the stake driven into daddy's heart at the end of that poem is the exorcising of a vampire that the prince, a combination of father and husband, has become, and it parallels the little mermaid's chance to regain her original form by using the enchanted knife her sisters had traded from the sea witch for their long hair.

Father and husband, Apollo and Dionysus, vampire and fairy-tale prince, muse and anti-muse: even here in *The Colossus*, a male image is often superimposed on the imagined world with which the speaker of the poems must interact. The other which stands for her world is often a colossal or imposing male figure identified with sea or stone. In the spring of 1958, Plath thought of titling this volume *Full Fathom Five*, saying that that title:

> relates more richly to my life and imagery than anything else I've dreamed up: has the background of *The Tempest*, the association of the sea, which is a central metaphor for my childhood, my poems and the artist's sub-conscious, of the father image—relating to my own father, the buried male muse and the god-creator risen to be my mate in Ted, to the sea—father Neptune—and the pearls and coral highly-wrought to art: pearls sea-changed from the ubiquitous grit of sorrow and dull routine. . . . —Oh, only left to myself, what a poet I will flay myself into. I shall begin by setting myself magic objects to write on: sea-bearded bodies— and begin thus, digging into the reaches of my deep submerged head, "and it's old and old it's sad and old it's sad and weary I go back to you, my cold father, my cold and father, my cold mad feary father . . ."— so Joyce says, so the river flows to the paternal source of godhead.[15]

In "Full Fathom Five," the other is imagined as yielding and dangerous because it can engulf the female narrator. In "Hardcastle Crags" the other is impervious to her and dangerous because she may be broken upon it. In "The Colossus," which she finally chose as the title poem of this volume, the other is an immense and formidable statue, probably based on the Colossus of Rhodes, of a male figure whom she again calls father.

Although the tone of "The Colossus" is one of rueful or wry humor, the poem finally concludes that at this point there is no longer any possibility of getting this image, which overshadows her own existence, put properly together. Right now the image, like that of the old man's face in "Full Fathom Five," clutters up her whole field of perception. "Your fluted bones and acanthine hair are littered / In their old anarchy to the horizon-line." In one sense, the poem documents a search for meaning, for a tradition she can fit into. The statue is in fragments and if she can somehow put it all together, rearrange it, not only will her task be completed and allow her to go on to something else, but she will have gained wisdom and some kind of definition of her own self from the labor. The image of the statue is, from the speaker's point of view, one of disjunction and cacophony rather than harmony and order.

> Mule-bray, pig-grunt and bawdy cackles
> Proceed from your great lips.
> It's worse than a barnyard.
>
> Perhaps you consider yourself an oracle,
> Mouthpiece of the dead, or of some god or other.

The center of the poem is the contrast between the statue and the woman. She is subordinated to it in size and significance. The landscape of her world is finally bounded by the statue: "The sun rises under the pillar of your tongue. / My hours are married to shadow." In fact, she has become so obsessed with this self-imposed task that she no longer even hopes for the possibility of a release: "No longer do I listen for the scrape of a keel / On the blank stones of the landing."

As a statue and reminiscent of Greek and Roman culture, the image of "The Colossus" records Sylvia Plath's confrontation with an overwhelmingly male tradition of which Virginia Woolf had earlier said, in a May 1903 letter to her brother Thoby, then at Cambridge:

I don't get anybody to argue with me now, & feel the want. I have to delve from books, painfully & all alone, what you get every evening sitting over your fire & smoking your pipe with Strachey, etc. No wonder my knowledge is but scant.[16]

Plath writes in her journal (December 27, 1958) about her feeling of "competing with Warren [her younger brother]: the looming image of Harvard is equated with him."[17]

While "Full Fathom Five" presents an image of the other that is a male figure superimposed upon the sea and "The Colossus" a stone male figure which is superimposed on the natural landscape, "Man in Black" (1959) carries this superimposition one step further. Here the fragments of both land and sea that make up the setting are drawn together and given meaning by a definitely human, though still abstract, figure. The man in black provides a center, a vortex, which connects all the disparate elements in the speaker's field of perception. One could see in this poem the capacity of the human to organize and give significance to experience, yet the figure in the poem does this primarily through being an imposition on the scene. The black he wears is more striking and overlays the grey sea, the dun headland, the ice, the snuff-colored sand cliffs, the white stones. All in all, he appears as a sinister figure. Plath says of this poem that "The 'dead black' . . . may be a transference from the visit to my father's grave" a month earlier.[18]

> And you, across those white
>
> Stones, strode out in your dead
> Black coat, black shoes, and your
> Black hair till there you stood,
>
> Fixed vortex on the far
> Tip, riveting stones, air,
> All of it, together.

The use of "dead" at the end of a line and as a stressed syllable to describe the color of his clothes, what is most significant about him, points toward the later poems, where death is what gives order and meaning to life and a possibility of perfection through an arresting of process. In a later poem, "Contusion," (*Ariel*), Plath uses the same technique of centering. "In a pit of rock / The sea sucks obsessively, / One hollow the whole sea's pivot." And in "The Eye Mote" (*The Colossus*), a lament for a lost innocence of vision, she writes: "Abrading my lid, the small grain burns: / Red cinder around which I myself, / Horses, planets and spires revolve." "The Colossus" and "Man in Black," centered on male figures which define and limit the poet's perception, both anticipate "Daddy," who begins that poem as a "ghastly statue with one grey toe / Big as a Frisco seal" and becomes a Gestapo officer, "a man in black with a Meinkampf look / And a love of the rack and the screw," and finally a vampire, an image which turns up increasingly in the later poems and includes her husband as well as her father.

The few poems in *The Colossus* which show a successful and creative interaction with the imaged world all have male personae. "Sculptor" (1958) and "Snakecharmer" (1957), the only two poems in this volume directly about the human as artist and creator, are both about men. Both the snakecharmer and the sculptor have an assured control of their world that the female personae of Plath's early poems never have. Both the sculptor and the snakecharmer are able to cross the boundaries and return with a vision which they seem to have no trouble communicating. Both are able to conquer and shape those elements which the female speakers of the poems cannot handle. The snakecharmer "pipes green. Pipes water," creates for his amusement "a world of snakes." The sculptor carves from bronze, wood, and stone his visions: "Until his chisel bequeaths / Them life livelier than ours, / A solider repose than death's." The only complete and successful transformation/apotheosis in *The Colossus* is "Faun" (1956), which has a male persona.

> An arena of yellow eyes
> Watched the changing shape he cut,
> Saw hoof harden from foot, saw sprout
> Goat-horns. Marked how god rose
> And galloped woodward in that guise.

The moles, frogs, and mushrooms which Plath has transformed herself into are all victims: dead, dying at the end of a season, or edible. None of those has the imperviousness or mobility that this faun achieves. And, while the personae of "Lorelei," "Full Fathom Five," and "Suicide Off Egg Rock" all want death by water, only the male persona of "Suicide Off Egg Rock" achieves a successful suicide.

This contrast is carried further in "Point Shirley" and "The Hermit at Outermost House," two 1959 poems which depict the struggle between human and nonhuman at a literal boundary. "The Hermit at Outermost House" is based on Henry Beston's *The Outermost House* (1928), his account of one year alone in a

cabin on Cape Cod. (Much of Plath's early work can be seen as
regional poetry based on Cape Cod and Boston.) The battle in
"The Hermit at Outermost House" is between the natural elements and the man. Aligned with nature is the supernatural—"the
great gods, Stone-Head, Claw-Foot"; they are opposed and in the
end routed by the same instrument the snakecharmer employs, "a
certain meaning green," and by the hermit's ability to laugh. Here
man is allied with sensuality, life, growth, green, and warmth,
and is opposed to sea, sky, and stone. But further, the hermit
beats these gods in league with the natural elements only by being
as hard and enduring as they are.

> For what, then, had they endured
> Dourly the long hots and colds,
> Those old despots, if he sat
>
> Laugh-shaken on his doorsill,
> Backbone unbendable as
> Timbers of his upright hut?

Plath says that "sky and sea . . . couldn't / Clapped shut, flatten
this man out" in contrast to a later poem, "Wuthering Heights"
(1961, *Crossing the Water*) which says in the first person: "The sky
leans on me, me, the one upright / Among all horizontals."

In "Point Shirley," Plath recalls her grandmother's efforts to
create a human environment at the very edge of the alien. She
"Kept house against / What the sluttish, rutted sea could do," a
task that required constant vigilance and unceasing effort. "She
wore her broom straws to the nub." What the sea could do, Plath
recounted elsewhere in her memory of the aftermath of a storm
when she was a child living near her grandmother in Winthrop
Beach, outside Boston.

> My final memory of the sea is of violence—a still, unhealthily yellow
> day in 1939, the sea molten, steely-slick, heaving at its leash like a broody
> animal, evil violets in its eye. . . .
> The wreckage the next day was all one could wish—overthrown trees
> and telephone poles, shoddy summer cottages bobbing out by the light-
> house and a litter of the ribs of little ships. My grandmother's house had
> lasted, valiant—though the waves broke right over the road and into the

bay. *My grandfather's seawall had saved it, neighbors said.* Sand buried her furnace in golden whorls; salt stained the upholstered sofa and a dead shark filled what had been the geranium bed, but my grandmother had her broom out, it would soon be right[19] [italics mine].

Though her grandmother is the heroic figure in "Point Shirley," in the time of the poem she has been dead twenty years. The poem is less about a heroic struggle that *is* (in a mythical present), like "The Hermit at Outermost House," than it is about a battle that was and has been lost. The other central figure in the poem is the poet, searching for her grandmother's strength which has been obliterated for so many years.

> A labour of love, and that labour lost.
> Steadily the sea
> Eats at Point Shirley. She died blessed,
> And I come by
> Bones, bones only, pawed and tossed,
> A dog-faced sea.

The housework which her grandmother performed was merely a holding action against destructive elements in contrast to the triumphant and more permanent creativity that characterizes the hermit, the snakecharmer, and the sculptor. What actually saved the house from the storm was her grandfather's sea wall. And in any case, the poem concludes, the grandmother's strength is not something that can be passed on to her granddaughter.

Sylvia Plath's movement in *The Colossus* poems out toward the boundaries, the attempted transformations into both animate and inanimate nature, are answered then by the male image which overshadows this first collection of poems. In "Hardcastle Crags," Plath had shown the woman in the poem caught between an alien nature and an alienating human world. In such a situation, representative of this whole first collection of poems, there is really no place for the self to go. "Watercolour of Grantchester Meadows" and "Mussel Hunter at Rock Harbor," the first in an English, the second in a New England setting, begin to show the self turning back into isolation.

"Watercolour of Grantchester Meadows" (1959) juxtaposes the

human romanticized concept of a natural scene with the far harsher reality. An apparent world of harmony, proportion, and peace, "It is a country on a nursery plate," suitable only for the naivety and innocence of childhood. "Arcadian green," it is arrested, beautiful, and benign. By the end of the third stanza, however, the reader begins to see that this is a facade: "The blood-berried hawthorn hides its spines with white." To see this scene as the stilled perfection of art, one needs a liberal helping of either ignorance or self-delusion, which the students provide as they

> . . . stroll or sit,
> Hands laced, in a moony indolence of love—
> Black-gowned, but unaware
> How in such mild air
> The owl shall stoop from his turret, the rat cry out.

"Mussel Hunter at Rock Harbor" (1958), places the speaking sensibility of the poem completely on the outside of a scene she can watch but never understand. Here the self is in the poem, though primarily as an observer she is conscious both of what is happening outside her and self-conscious of her own reaction. The poem is a recognition of the final and complete separation between herself and what she observes, which seems to her utterly alien and incomprehensible.

> The mussels hung dull blue and
> Conspicuous, yet it seemed
> A sly world's hinges had swung
> Shut against me.

The poem is based on an experience in August 1957 when she observed fiddler crabs, "an evil cross between spiders and lobsters and crickets," during a vacation on Cape Cod. She describes the scene in her journal in careful detail, ending "An image: weird, of another world with its own queer habits, of mud, lumped, underpeopled with quiet crabs."[20] The description of the fiddler crabs which makes up most of the poem is clearly an attempt by the human mind to give meaning to something outside human understanding. She images them as knights, as hordes, watches them move with a purpose she cannot understand. Then she asks a question which indicates she is trying to impose human considerations on them and just as quickly realizes its absurdity.

> . . . Could they feel mud
> Pleasurable under claws
>
> As I could between bare toes?
> That question ended it—I
> Stood shut out, for once, for all,
> Puzzling the passage of their
> Absolutely alien
> Order

The speaker of the poem notes but deliberately avoids discussion of the huge claw which serves as weapon. "But grown grimly, and grimly / Borne, for a use beyond my / Guessing of it." Though able, to some extent, to identify with the frogs, moles and mushrooms in her poems which are victims, she cannot identify with the predatory crabs. When she tries to look at herself from the crabs' point of view, the result is curiously flat: "From what the crabs saw, / If they could see, I was one / Two-legged mussel-picker." It would be bad enough merely if the self were shut out, could not pass the boundaries, were defined by the flatness of this final image in "Mussel Hunter at Rock Harbor." But not only is the self driven back into isolation, she must, trapped, watch figures from the world of nightmare themselves cross the boundaries and invade what we think of as reality.

"The Disquieting Muses" (1957) contrasts the world of mundane reality represented by the speaker's mother and another world inhabited by the three ladies who nod by night around her bed. The battle between these two worlds for possession of the speaker of the poem has been going on since infancy. They stand: "With heads like darning-eggs to nod / And nod and nod at foot and head / And at the left side of my crib?" Their major characteristic is silence. In their "gowns of stone" they are kin to the Lorelei, but the tone of this poem is more ominous. They are figures of sensory deprivation. The disquieting muses have no visible sense receptors. Their heads are like "darning-eggs"; they are "mouthless, eyeless, with stitched bald head." They are malevolent, sent, like the bad fairy in "Sleeping Beauty," as a curse and moreover as a result of her mother's negligence.

> Mother, Mother, what illbred aunt
> Or what disfigured and unsightly
> Cousin did you so unwisely keep
> Unasked to my christening, that she
> Sent these ladies in her stead

It is clear throughout the poem that the frightening figures of the disquieting muses are truer, more real, than the comforting but illusory world her mother represents. It is characteristic of Plath's poetry that the dark, the horrifying, and the unexpected is seen through the ordinary, the mundane, the expected, as though the dark is not even the other side of the same coin but rather as if the ordinary and the expected are so thin, almost transparent in places, that the dark shows through. The speaker's mother always tried to cover up what lurked behind the ordinary. Sometimes she tried to exorcise it, to dispel fear; more often she pretended it did not exist, and this last is what the speaker of the poem cannot forgive.

The first stanza of the poem evokes these stony figures. The four stanzas that follow present four incidents, instances of her mother's world and her mother's effort to keep her in that world, a world where "witches always, always / Got baked into gingerbread," where cookies and ovaltine and chorused invocations kept off the gods who brought storm. But always she sees instead the figures of her disquieting muses successfully moving across the boundaries, invading the everyday world, like the sea in "Point Shirley" encroaching on the land. The speaker's mother here, as in *The Bell Jar*, is seen as the agent of her daughter's socialization and there is a great deal of resentment directed at her. The fourth and fifth stanzas recount incidents where her mother tried to involve her in the sort of school activities young girls are traditionally supposed to enjoy: a school dance production and piano lessons. Her mother lied, she says,

> praised my arabesques and trills
> Although each teacher found my touch

Oddly wooden in spite of scales
And the hours of practicing, my ear
Tone-deaf and yes, unteachable.

Each stanza ends with a reassertion of the presence of these stone-gowned figures and of the failure of her mother's world to hold her. Stanza six documents its final defeat. Her mother (and other women of her generation) exist in a kind of Walt Disney world which is here seen as manifestly unreal.

I work one day to see you, mother
Floating above me in bluest air
On a green balloon bright with a million
Flowers and bluebirds that never were
Never, never, found anywhere.

Her mother bobs away on this soap bubble world, and finally the speaker faces her "traveling companions." And now, they are with her all the time. They are blank, they are stone, they exist in a twilight realm where the "setting sun / . . . never brightens or goes down." In the last lines of the poem, she reasserts her opening blame of her mother; it is her mother's fault she has had to turn to this blank world.

Why is there such resentment and anger against her mother in this poem and against older women in general in *The Bell Jar*? I think Plath, and many other young women in post–World War II America, saw in their own lives what Wilhelm Reich had noted in his study of Hitler's Germany, *The Mass Psychology of Fascism*: Women traditionally have been the agents of the transmission of ideology to the next generation, often transmitting an ideology thoroughly opposed to their own interests and to their daughters'. Thus he shows that facism, a middle class movement which placed the preservation of the authoritarian nuclear family at the center of its program, "relied chiefly upon women's votes."[21] And he quotes Hitler in a 1932 proclamation:

No matter how far woman's sphere of activity can be stretched, the ultimate aim of a truly organic and logical development must always be the creation of a family. It is the smallest but most valuable unit in the complete structure of the state. Work honors both man and woman. But the child exalts the woman.[22]

Forced to identify with and live up to a primarily male fantasy of herself, woman in Nazi Germany and postwar America both becomes a perpetrator of ideology because, were it demystified, she would lose the only identity she has. A major characteristic of Fascist ideology was the sentimentality produced by this idealization of woman as mother in order to maintain the authoritarian nuclear family structure. The harshness that is the actual fact of woman's place is masked by sentimentality, a disparity between an event or situation and the emotion attached to that event or situation. Sentimentality, in focusing overmuch on the subject, allows one to be self-indulgent, selfish, and self-deluded. The mother in "The Disquieting Muses" is seen as selfish in her attempt to create in the daughter a mirror image of herself.[23] Certainly she is seen by the speaker of the poem as self-deluding. The attempt to socialize the daughter is rejected in this poem, as it is in *The Bell Jar* where the protagonist's mother is portrayed with even more bitterness. The speaker of this poem flees from a world seen as dangerously false behind its saccharine surface into a self-imposed blankness. The sensory deprivation suggested here by the featureless darning-egg heads of her muses, symbol of her poetic voice, anticipate the vacuum of the bell jar, where one is "blank as a stopped baby," as well as the final transformation in *The Colossus* into a stone.[24]

"The Thin People" (1957) also presents nightmare figures from another world encroaching upon the world of everyday reality it borders. But what was a personal situation in "The Disquieting Muses" becomes explicitly social in "The Thin People." And while the disquieting muses are not wholly unwelcomed—at least they are real where her mother's world is false—the thin people (referred to as "they" throughout) are seen entirely as threat. The tone of the poem is guilty, as though the speaker of the poem had helped to cause their thinness.

What characterizes the thin people is their silence, their accusing malevolence, and their lack of color. The movement in Sylvia Plath's poems is toward a world in stark black and white, with splashes of red. The thin people, however, bring grey. They stand in opposition to the world of the senses with its warmth and vibrant color. Their menace is nothing overt or obtrusive, "but a thin silence." One of the first of Plath's poems with an overtly historical/economic context and imagery, it forms a bridge to the imaged social world of the *Ariel* poems. The thin people are victims and an externalization of social guilt, who remain to haunt those who have forgotten their own crimes against them and are fat again. The world is haunted by spectors who are victims of public and private oppression. They have an effect on the living or at least on the speaker of the poem, who sees them as constant background to what we usually think of as the real.

"The Thin People" is the first of Plath's poems specifically identifying human victims, and moreover, victims as members of a class. The world imaged in the poem is a contemporary social world; the reference to a movie screen comes as a shock to readers used, in *The Colossus*, to trees, rocks, wind, and sea. Plath specifically identifies the thin people as victims of the Second World War: "It was only / In a war making evil headlines when we / Were small." They are martyrs and their silence is accusing. They began as real, faded away into dreams and the archives of forgotten documentary films; now, because of the poet's acceptance of social guilt, they come back from nightmare into daylight.

> Now the thin people do not obliterate
> Themselves as the dawn
> Grayness blues, reddens, and the outline
> Of the world comes clear and fills with
> color.
> They persist in the sunlit room.

They persist and make everything else grow thin as they are. Unlike the disquieting muses and the ancestors in "All the Dead Dears" who want to pull her into their realm (the eternal envy and enmity of the dead for the living, a variant of the vampire imagery of her later poems), the thin people's "stiff battalions" advance, like the encroaching sea in "Point Shirley," inexorably into the everyday world. And their effect is to thin out the world, to absorb and negate all color and warmth. The interpolated story of the old woman who sliced the moon up for food until nothing was left, although it has a fairy-tale charm, also indicates the hunger of the thin people for life, for an acknowledged existence.

When social explanations for events are repressed, they have a tendency to turn inward and become psychological, both as explanation and as response. Thus paranoia, for example, if repressed as social reality, will reappear in individuals as a psychological problem or "abnormality." A black radical leader once said that while paranoia may be a psychological abnormality for a white person in America, for a black man or woman it is a social reality. Similarly, while for a white male in America, schizophrenia may be a psychological abnormality, for a woman it has been a reality based on the doubly bound conditions of her everyday life: of being defined rather than defining herself, of being defined in contradictory ways. Phyllis Chesler, in her discussion of Ellen West, Elizabeth Packard, Zelda Fitzgerald, and Sylvia Plath in *Woman and Madness*, says:

All four women existed under a "bell jar"—both inside and outside the asylum. For them, madness and confinement were both an expression of female powerlessness and an unsuccessful attempt to overcome this state. Madness and asylums generally function as mirror images of the female experience, and as penalties for *being* "female," as well as for daring *not* to be. If the dare is enacted deeply or dramatically enough, death (through slow or fast suicide) ensues.[25]

Some background to the parallels between the self-image of women diagnosed as schizophrenic and incarcerated in asylums and the self-image of psychologically "normal" women in America in the 20-year period following the end of World War II is suggested by the disparity between the rise in women's expectations during the war and the squashing of those same expectations after the war when women were turned out of their jobs and back into the house to make room for returning soldiers. This rapid shift in attitude about women's place was hardest on adolescent girls and young women, whose expectations about what they could professionally accomplish were shaped during the war years. William Chafe, in *The American Woman: Her Changing Social, Economic and Political Role, 1920–1970*, writes that "of 33,000 girl students sampled in a *Senior Scholastic* poll [in 1945], 88 percent wanted a career in addition to homemaking, while only 4 percent chose homemaking exclusively." At the same time, he reports, the movement to push women back into their houses was already accelerating.

Frieda Miller, chief of the Women's Bureau, observed that public opinion had shifted from a period of "excessive admiration for women's capacity to do anything, over to the idea . . . that women ought to be delighted to give up any job and return to their proper sphere—the kitchen." Even those women leaders who had been most skeptical of the gains made in wartime were stunned by the toboggan in public esteem.[26]

A crisis of identity occurred for American women in the 1950s, which Betty Friedan in *The Feminine Mystique* suggests was caused by the existence of public and official images of women which were inimical to personal growth and which at the same time precluded, except in the most fortunate, a private image that would sustain the individual from day to day.[27]

The search for a self-image true to one's own sense of one's potentiality, when thwarted by external and internalized social restrictions, can take distorted and ambiguous forms. "The Stones," one of the latest poems included in *The Colossus*, is described by Ted Hughes as "clearly enough the first eruption of the voice that produced *Ariel*. It is the poem where the self, shattered in 1953, suddenly finds itself whole."[28] Plath herself later dismissed everything prior to "The Stones" as juvenilia. "Poem for a Birthday," of which "The Stones" is the seventh and final section, was written when Plath was pregnant with her first child, and it is true that the poem is in part about this sense of imminent birth, of restless anticipation. But the birthday anticipated in the poem is also for herself, and the kind of images used to describe that birth are foreshadowed by the earlier incomplete and unsuccessful attempts at metamorphosis which appear throughout *The Colossus*.

The first section of "Poem for a Birthday," called "Who," introduces the theme of unobtrusiveness and passivity, the desire to be unnoticed and therefore not have to deal with the complexity of living.[29] "Let me sit in a flowerpot," she writes. "The spiders won't notice. / My heart is a stopped geranium." And later in the same section what the poem as a whole will lead to becomes clear:

"I am a root, a stone, an owl pellet, / Without dreams of any sort." In "Maenad," the third section of "Poem for a Birthday," the speaker of the poem says, "When it thundered I hid under a flat stone," and in the sixth section, "Witch Burning": "If I am a little one, I can do no harm. / If I don't move about, I'll knock nothing over. So I said, / Sitting under a potlid, tiny and inert as a rice grain." "The Stones," the culmination of "Poem for a Birthday," takes place in "the city where men are mended." The self becomes "a still pebble" and is purified and made blank: "Sponges kiss my lichens away." Also described as "the stomach of indifference, the wordless cupboard," this interim state is a place beyond human concerns, beyond language. Earlier, in "Who," she had written "For weeks I can remember nothing at all," and "Maenad" ends "Tell me my name."

Like "Hardcastle Crags," the final section of "Poem for a Birthday" is about the confrontation of the human and the nonhuman imaged as stone. All of "Poem for a Birthday" posits the self as becoming part of this other realm. Unlike "Hardcastle Crags," where the woman turned back "before the weight / Of stones and hills of stones could break / Her down to mere quartz grit in that stony light," in "Who" she says "Mother of otherness / Eat me." In "Hardcastle Crags" the self was in danger of being destroyed by the sheer otherness, the alienness of the world around her, a nature that was impervious to her and upon which she could leave no trace. In "The Stones," the speaking sensibility of *The Colossus* poems becomes not necessarily a part of nature or the other, but like it, alien and impervious. Those qualities that had been seen as frightening and dangerous in the 1956 "Hardcastle Crags" are by 1959 taken on by the self as a defense. R. D. Laing, in *The Divided Self*, writes:

It seems to be a general law that at some point those very dangers most dreaded can themselves be encompassed to forestall their actual occurrence. Thus, to forego one's autonomy becomes the means of secretly safeguarding it; to play possum, to feign death, becomes a means of preserving one's aliveness. . . . To turn oneself into a stone becomes a way of not being turned into a stone by someone else.[30]

Laing equated petrification or the act of turning someone into a stone or turning oneself into a stone with depersonalization. It is, he says, the act whereby one negates the other person's autonomy, ignores his feel-ings, regards him as a thing, kills the life in him. In this sense one may perhaps better say that one depersonalizes him, or reifies him. One treats him not as a person, as a free agent, but as an it.[31]

In one of the *Ariel* poems, "The Rival," (1961) the speaker of the poem writes of her husband: "Your first gift is making stone out of everything." In "Poem for a Birthday" what is being objecti-fied, depersonalized, and reified is the "I" of the poem.

"The Stones" also can be seen as the first of Sylvia Plath's hos-pital poems, a setting that occurs with increasing frequency in her poetry after 1959. In "Two Views of a Cadaver Room" (1959), also in *The Colossus*, the speaker is an observer. But in "The Stones" and later pieces like "Paralytic" (1963), "Tulips" (1961), and the verse play *Three Women* (1962), the perspective is from the inside: the subject of the poem is a patient, helpless, an object, moved about and acted upon by others. Even though the woman in "The Stones," like the speaker of "Tulips," is going to leave the hos-pital—she says at the end of the poem "My mendings itch.There is nothing to do. / I shall be good as new"—nevertheless the poem emphasizes a world in which she does not have control over her own body. By turning herself into (or letting herself be turned into) a stone, which is relatively impervious to outside effects and yet cannot move, cannot see, cannot speak, cannot feel, she si-multaneously is and is not an object of the control of others.

Laing quotes extensively in *The Divided Self* from a case history reported by two American psychiatrists, M. L. Hayward and J. E. Taylor ("A schizophrenic patient describes the action of intensive psychotherapy," 1956). The self-image of this patient, also an American, significantly parallels Sylvia Plath's. "Joan is a twenty-six-year-old white woman. Her illness first appeared early in 1947 when she was seventeen. . . . Three suicide attempts were made, by slashing herself with broken glass or taking an overdose of sedation." Joan was born in 1930, two years before Sylvia Plath; she is twenty-six at the time these quotes were recorded in 1956, the beginning of the three-year period during which Plath wrote *The Colossus* poems. Joan says, "I felt as though I were in a bottle. I could feel that everything was outside and couldn't touch me."[32]

Laing quotes a poem written by this female patient which has a number of parallels to Plath's poems in terms of images of self, of world, and interaction between self and world. Joan speaks of being imprisoned in a cave with "stony sides," "only black depth," and "almost no air." She is not alone but surrounded by "large, enormous" people who "echo themselves when they talk" and sometimes step on her, by mistake she hopes, crushing her into the cave walls, and transforming her. "I shall become part of the cave walls," she writes, and "I shall be an echo and a shadow." The sense of being overwhelmed, of being imprisoned in a stuffy, airless, and enclosed place, the sense that others are larger and have greater substantiality than oneself, and finally the defense, which is to become part of the cave walls, hard, immovable, and impervious to outside effects, are all very similar to the recurring images in Sylvia Plath's poetry between 1956 and 1959.

But what is particularly interesting is that this sense of suffocation, smallness, and immobility is also a part of the self-image of many American women in the 1950s who were considered sane, secure, and happy with their homes and children. Betty Friedan, from her study of women's magazines in the 1950s, asks:

Does it say something about the new housewife readers that, as any editor can testify, they can identify completely with the victims of blindness, deafness, physical maiming, cerebral palsy, paralysis, cancer, or approaching death? Such articles about people who cannot see or speak or move have been an enduring staple of the women's magazines in the era of "Occupation: housewife."[33]

That the conditions with which the average American woman since 1945 can identify are not only immobilizing but possibly incurable is suggested in both Joan's attempt to explain herself and in Sylvia Plath's "The Stones." Though Plath says here, as Esther Greenwood does at the end of The Bell Jar, that she will be "good as new," the rest of the imaged experience undercuts the optimistic final statement. In "The Stones," the speaker of the poem says: "The vase, reconstructed, houses / The elusive rose. / Ten fingers shape a bowl for shadows." Her attitude toward her cure is ambivalent. It is possible that all the repair that has been done to her in this poem has been done to the outside; the real self, shadowy and elusive, may be still untouched.

What the presumed repair and the transformation into a stone have accomplished is to finally fix and rigidify the outer limits of the boundaries between self and other. Throughout *The Colossus* there has been attempt after attempt to become part of this otherness, to cross the borders into the unknown and there find a self redefined with which she can merge and be truly reborn—and then, like the hero of Campbell's monomyth, to bring that reborn self back across the boundaries into this world. What has happened instead is that the borders have progressively shifted inward as the sea erodes Point Shirley, as images of her dead ancestors "reach hag hands to haul me in," (All the Dead Dears) as the thin people's stiff battalions move from sleeping into waking nightmare. The task of the later poetry is to explore the shrinking limits of the bounded and enclosed world in which she now knows she lives.

NOTES

1. Karl Marx, "The Eighteenth Brumaire of Louis Bonaparte," in *The Marx-Engels Reader*, ed. Robert C. Tucker (New York: W. W. Norton, 1972), p. 437. (Originally published in 1852).

2. Virginia Woolf, *A Room of One's Own* (New York: Harcourt, Brace & World, 1929), p. 79.

3. Joseph Campbell, *Hero with a Thousand Faces* (New York: World Publishing, 1949), pp. 37–38.

4. Ibid., pp. 39–40.

5. Northrop Frye, in Norton lectures at Harvard University, 4/17/75.

6. W. B. Yeats, *The Collected Poems of W. B. Yeats* (New York: Macmillan, 1933).

7. Carolyn G. Heilbrun, "Presidential Address 1984" in *PMLA*, Vol. 100, No. 3, pp. 281–82.

8. Ted Hughes, "Notes on the Chronological Order of Sylvia Plath's Poems" in *The Art of Sylvia Plath*, p. 191.

9. Sylvia Plath, *The Bell Jar* (New York: Harper & Row, 1971), pp. 126–31.

10. Sylvia Plath, *The Journals of Sylvia Plath*, (New York: Dial Press, 1982), pp. 245–46.

11. Kate Chopin, *The Awakening* (New York: Avon, 1972), p. 189.

12. "Sleeping Beauty," in *Household Stories by the Brothers Grimm*, trans. by Lucy Crane (New York: Dover, 1963), pp. 204–7.

13. Hans Christian Anderson, "The Little Mermaid" in *Hans Christian*

Anderson: The Complete Fairy Tales and Stories, trans. by Erik Christian Haugaard (New York: Doubleday, 1974), pp. 57–76.

14. Plath, *Journal*, p. 219.

15. Ibid., p. 223 (May 11, 1958).

16. Quoted in Quentin Bell, *Virginia Woolf: A Biography* (New York: Harcourt, Brace, Jovanovich, 1972), p. 70.

17. Plath, *Journal*, p. 281.

18. Ibid., p. 302 (April 23, 1959).

19. Sylvia Plath, "Ocean 1212-W" in *Johnny Panic and The Bible of Dreams*, pp. 25–26.

20. Plath, *Journal*, p. 174.

21. Wilhelm Reich, *The Mass Psychology of Fascism* (New York: Simon and Schuster, 1969), pp. 106–7.

22. Ibid., p. 61.

23. In her journal (December 1958), at the time she is doing therapy with Dr. Ruth Beuscher, Plath talks about freeing herself from her mother and the other older women in her life (such as Mary Ellen Chase, a teacher at Smith who had encouraged her) whose expectations make her guilty and fearful. She says (to herself): "You think all old women are magical witches" (p. 290). She says: "My mother had sacrificed her life for me. A sacrifice I didn't want" (p. 269). She says:

> I felt I couldn't write because she [her mother] would appropriate it. Is that all? I felt if I didn't write nobody would accept me as a human being. Writing, then, was a substitute for myself: If you don't love me, love my writing and love me for my writing. . . . When I am cured of my witch-belief, I will be able to tell her of writing without a flinch and still feel it is mine! (p. 281).

24. Plath, *The Bell Jar*, p. 193.

25. Phyllis Chesler, *Women and Madness* (New York: Doubleday, 1972), pp. 15–16.

26. William H. Chafe, *The American Woman: Her Changing Social, Economic, and Political Role, 1920–1970* (New York: Oxford University Press, 1972), pp. 178, 179.

27. Betty Friedan, *The Feminine Mystique* (New York: Dell, 1963). See especially Chapter Three, "The Crisis in Women's Identity," pp. 62–72.

28. Ted Hughes, "Notes on the Chronological Order of Sylvia Plath's Poems," p. 192.

29. Richard Howard has called this the "Lithic impulse—the desire, the need to reduce the demands of life to the unquestioning acceptance of a stone" in "Sylvia Plath: 'And I Have No Face, I Have Wanted to Efface Myself.' " in *The Art of Sylvia Plath*, p. 79.

30. R. D. Laing, *The Divided Self* (Middlesex, England: Penguin, 1965), p. 51.

31. Ibid., p. 46.

32. Ibid., Chapter 10, "The Self and the False Self in a Schizophrenic," pp. 160–77.

33. Friedan, *The Feminine Mystique*, p. 46.

~ 3 ~

Speech and Silence: The Transitional Poetry

Already in *The Colossus*, there are suggestions that the world of the poems is becoming more enclosed: "a sly world's hinges had swung / Shut against me" ("Mussel Hunter at Rock Harbor"). The poems from the period 1959–62, many of them originally collected in *Crossing the Water* (1971), document a movement from a world of fluidity and potentiality to a world seen as increasingly rigid and narrow.[1] Possibilities are closed off; boundaries between self and world have solidified. As Plath moves toward the *Ariel* poems, she no longer becomes in her poetry some aspect of animate or inanimate nature. What had before been animistically projected outward onto the natural world is now internalized as Plath faces the social world.[2] Rather than a projection of self outward, she begins to feel trapped inside the self. This shift in perception is further demonstrated in where Plath locates the alien and threatening. What was in the early poems seen as being alien and outside her moves to being alien and inside her. In "Hardcastle Crags" (*The Colossus*) the sleepwalking woman confronts a world of primal stone "unaltered by eyes," so alien to herself as to be incomprehensible. But there is a hint even in this early poem that the woman partakes of this alienness. She too has some of the qualities of stone, albeit an inferior sort. By "The Stones" at the end of *The Colossus*, the speaking sensibility of the poems has begun to internalize the alien that she has earlier found mostly outside herself and a threat. She has metaphorically become a stone, impervious in the sense that she does not need to react to the world around her; she can lie passive and indifferent. This progressive internalization of the alien continues into a poem like "Elm" in *Ariel*, where the alien is seen as living inside her. "I am terrified by this dark thing / That sleeps in me; / All day I feel its soft, feathery turnings, its malignity."

The change in Plath's poetic voice and the transformation of her central images are both tied to a change in her conception of self-image, image of the world, and relation between self and world. This developing awareness of self is exemplified most clearly in Plath's suspicion of language. In a late poem, "Words" (*Ariel*), she compares language to the echoes of axe strokes that hide the bleeding of sap from a tree and to ripples of water that conceal a skull-like sunken rock. These metaphors could be seen as an expression of the natural concern of a poet that she be listened to, but I think they indicate as well a much deeper suspicion about the relationship of an artisan whose tools are words to the substance with which she is trying to work.

If language is a reflection of one's culture, if its structure is based on the assumptions of that culture, a poet uncomfortable with those assumptions is likely to feel uncomfortable with language as well. Language structures our perceptions of self and other: In the act of labeling, it tells us what to see and what not to see; through its syntax, it tells us what the relations are between the things we do see. As a woman poet trying to work out a redefinition of self through her poetry, Plath found herself in a linguistic trap. If she accepted her language without question, she would be accepting a set of assumptions which devalued her, confused her about her priorities, and limited her sense of personal possibility. As a consequence of this dilemma, what begins to develop in these middle poems is a suspicion about the nature and function of language itself and the beginnings of an analysis of the connection between language and society. In both imagery and in attitude toward language in these transitional poems, the sense of entrapment is crucial.

This transition from one set of images to another, from a dialectic of self and nature to a dialectic of self and history in which mythology continues to play a crucial role, is clear in "Barren

Woman" (1961), a poem originally published in *Crossing the Water* with the title "Small Hours." Sterility, especially female biological inability to bear children, becomes a crucial metaphor in the post-*Colossus* poems for stasis, entrapment, the noncreative, an end to process. The character of the Secretary in *Three Women* is the most fully realized incarnation of this figure in Plath's Gallery of Masks. The barren woman is not only a powerful archetype, it is also a critical response to a real situation in which female biological creativity is valued more highly than any other kind of female creativity. In "Barren Woman," set in the small hours of the night, the speaker of the poem sees both the world and herself as blank and empty. The poem describes an internal landscape. The self, isolated, wanders through this landscape, which is littered with the symbols she had previously used (in *The Colossus* poems) to image her internal state. In the first stanza, she describes herself as an empty museum. "Empty, I echo to the least footfall, / Museum without statues, grand with pillars, porticoes, rotundas." Everything is static, motionless, except the fountain which seems at first to offer some possibility of movement: "In my courtyard a fountain leaps and sinks back into itself." Like the grasses in "Hardcastle Crags," which also initially seemed to offer some possibility of movement and life in a stone-frozen world but were really "tied, as a moonbound sea / Moves on its root," the fountain in "Small Hours" also becomes an image of restriction, of deceptive or aborted energy. It "leaps and sinks back into itself, / Nun-hearted and blind to the world." The paralleling of "nun-hearted" and "blind" helps explain the recurrent references to purity in *The Bell Jar* and the *Ariel* poems. Purity implies sensory deprivation, blindness, stoniness, stasis, and sterility. Finally, there is only the illusion of movement in "Barren Woman," for the fountain is caught in an enclosed cycle. It is essentially static.

The increasing concern with stasis in the later poetry is an aspect of Sylvia Plath's feeling of entrapment, that there is no place to get to. Her attitude toward stasis is ambiguous. On the one hand, it would be comfortable, an end to the multidirectional energy engendered by hope and frustration, to just stop, to assume indifference; to become, like some of her earlier images of nature, impervious to the effects of the world around her. Stasis also suggests stability. On the other hand, to stop means to remain with the unsatisfactory definition of self she now has. And the growing recognition that whatever she may want, her position is in fact closed and static, leads to an increasing sense in the last poems that the moment of anguish is "stopped" and eternal.

The speaker of "Barren Woman" sees herself as a museum without statues. The colossus who stood for her father and who overshadowed the world of her first collection of poems is still there, but he has been transformed from a mythic and motionless image of her past to a more dynamic and therefore more threatening part of her contemporary social reality; the change is also from a parent figure, something that engendered her, to something she is mother of and herself creates. In the second stanza of "Barren Woman" Plath moves rather abruptly to the new set of images: "I imagine myself with a great public, / Mother of a white Nike and several bald-eyed Apollos." The "bald-eyed Apollos" are a transitional image. Clearly they refer both to classical statues and to a modern series of missiles, equipped with warheads, like the Nike tested in the late 1950s. The change, then, is to a contemporary world and, while the image of missiles does suggest a potential power in her, yet its obvious link with destructiveness if immediately, if glancingly, recognized: "The dead injure me with attentions." The movement in "Barren Woman," then, is from a recognition of emptiness, futility, blindness, and stasis to an imagined possibility of strength, power, activity, and purpose—which missiles undeniably have. It is also a movement from human creation to human destruction, and from human creation engendering human destruction toward a recognition that her social reality is dominated by patriarchal values and modes of action. "That flat, flat, flatness from which ideas, destructions, / Bulldozers, guillotines, white chambers of shrieks proceed" says the second voice in *Three Women*. Plath's simultaneous acceptance and rejection of these values results in an ambivalent attitude. To be successful, Plath, like many women coming to adulthood in the 1950s, accepted her father as role model; her writing demonstrates, part of the time, a resultant contempt for the weak and victimized and a yearning for the power which should go along with the success she fought so hard for. On the other hand, the recognition of her socially defined role as woman, with its emphasis on female creativity as biological, turns the indoctrinated contempt into self-contempt. For a woman poet, biological barrenness can become a metaphor for aesthetic barrenness, and in any case what is created may be dangerous and an instrument leading to death. I am reminded of Ellen Moers's brilliant analysis of Mary Shelley's *Frankenstein* as a "horror story of maternity," based on Shelley's own experiences with miscarriages and stillbirths. Moers writes: "The sources of this Gothic conception . . . were surely the anxieties of a woman who, as daughter, mistress, and mother, was a bearer of death."[3]

Sylvia Plath's sense of being trapped is grounded in a realization of, among other things, the rigidity of sex roles. In *The Bell Jar*, written in the same two-year period as the later poetry, she writes:

Buddy Willard was always saying how his mother said, "What a man wants is a mate and what a woman wants is infinite security," and "What a man is is an arrow into the future and what a woman is is the place the arrow shoots off from."[4]

The last thing I wanted was infinite security and to be the place an arrow shoots off from. I wanted change and excitement and to shoot off in all directions myself, like the colored arrows from a Fourth of July rocket (p. 68).

I was so scared, as if I were being stuffed farther and farther into a black, airless sack with no way out (p. 105).

Esther Greenwood's response to being trapped is similar to that of the speaker of "Barren Woman," who pulls back from her vision of potential power and destruction, back into a static world where, if there is no movement, there is at least no annihilation: "nothing can happen." The blankness returns and she is touched by another avatar of her disquieting muses, who bring the silence of sensory deprivation: "The moon lays a hand on my forehead, / Blank-faced and mum as a nurse."

"Barren Woman" has a transitional place in Sylvia Plath's poetry similar to "A Coat" (*Responsibilities*, 1914) in Yeats's poetry. Both poems are a summing up of past images and concerns, and an announcement, Plath's more indirect, of a new approach. Yeats says of his earlier poetry:

I made my song a coat
Covered with embroideries

Out of old mythologies
From heel to throat.[5]

But now, he writes: "there's more enterprise / In walking naked."
The poetry that immediately follows becomes increasingly social,
indeed political, and his voice, like Plath's in the poetry after *The
Colossus*, increasingly direct and unadorned with "old mythologies."

The connection between Plath and Yeats is an odd one: She
died in a house in London where Yeats had once lived. One of
the major tensions in Plath's poetry (between engagement and disengagement) parallels Yeats' major concern. As Margaret Dickie
Uroff says, "If Plath sometimes sounds like Hughes, it is because
they both sound like Yeats."[6] The personae of his poetry balance
between being of this world and not of it, between the turbulence
of unordered passion and the static perfection of art, between living and dying. In December 1962, just two months before she
committed suicide, Plath wrote to a friend:

A small miracle happened—I'd been to Yeats' tower at Ballylea while in
Ireland and thought it the most beautiful and peaceful place in the world;
then walking desolately around my beloved Primrose Hill in London and
brooding on the hopelessness of ever finding a flat. . . . I passed Yeats'
house, with its plaque 'Yeats lived here' which I'd often passed and longed
to live in. A signboard was up—flats to rent, I flew to the agent. By a
miracle you can only know if you've ever tried to flat hunt in London, I
was the first to apply. . . . I am here on a five year lease and it is utter
heaven. . . . And it's Yeats' house, which right now means a lot to me.[7]

Though his poetry is full of the conflict between wanting to live
and wanting to stop, Yeats grasped more at life the closer he got
to death, realizing even from within the elaborate symbol system
of *A Vision* that the timeless, static perfection of art is not possible
without the imperfection, the process, the very temporality of life.
Metaphors for poetry come from life, from "the foul rag-and-
bone shop of the heart."

For Sylvia Plath, struggling with similar conflicts, settling in
Yeats's house must have seemed an auspicious sign. However,
Yeats had something to tie him to this life, a tradition he could

look back to and identify with, the heroic past of Irleand; and he could become involved in his own life with an attempt to reforge that tradition in the present through the Irish theater. Sylvia Plath was in a more closed situation. Like many modern American poets, she had little sense of a living and viable past to give the present meaning. One of Plath's teachers, Robert Lowell, wrote in "Concord": "Ten thousand Fords are idle here in search of a tradition." Lowell's cars, while they suggest the mechanization, dehumanization, and ahistoricism of contemporary American society and particularly the situation of the American artist in the 1950s, nevertheless have a certain charm. And Lowell finally does succeed in finding a family tradition of sorts. But for Plath, family history holds either terror—her ancestors "reach hag hands to haul me in" ("All the Dead Dears")—or lies, as in the speaker's characterization of her mother in "The Disquieting Muses" (*The Colossus*). Neither can she find a tradition in American history, which she feels has been at best complicity in exploitation, and for which she accepts her own measure of social guilt. Not only as an American but also as a woman artist Sylvia Plath was in a more closed situation than Yeats. For while Yeats could identify with Ireland's heroic past, both in history and myth, of battles fought and maidens won, as a woman Sylvia Plath could find no comparable tradition in language, literature, and history, through which she could define herself.

Plath's suspicion of language as a vehicle for a male-dominated literary tradition and her more general, though indirect, antagonism toward language as something which traps her through misdefining her, begins to emerge in "Two Campers in Cloud Country" (1960), and is further developed in "Crossing the Water" (1962), both based on a camping trip Plath and Hughes took in the summer of 1959. That she now perceives her world as social is apparent, for both these poems center on a confrontation between the two campers, who are representatives of society, and the alien and therefore dangerous natural environment surrounding them. In both poems a silent battle is waged between social qualities of order, rationality, the need to control, and especially the need to name, between this social world represented by the two campers, who are in "Crossing the Water" described as "black, cut-paper people," and the natural world, arational, noncontrolled, out of the control specifically of language, overpowering. In "Two Campers in Cloud Country," she writes: "In this country there is neither measure nor balance / To redress the dominance of rocks and woods." There are no "labeled elms" or "tame tea-roses." Instead there is the danger of language slipping away entirely and, with it, the magic control of one's surroundings that is peculiarly human. "No gesture of yours or mine could catch their attention, / No word make them carry water or fire the kindling / Like local trolls in the spell of a superior being." In fact, faced with this disordered immensity, the human is no longer superior. As in "The Colossus," where the speaker could not attach meaning to and therefore control the image of the statue, the contrast in "Two Campers in Cloud Country" is between the immensity of nature and the puniness of the human. The clouds are "man-shaming," the horizons "far off"; the "colors assert themselves," and "night arrives in one gigantic step." In such an environment, the chief activity of the two campers is to bolster each other's very existence. "I lean to you, numb as a fossil. Tell me I'm here." But it doesn't work.

> The pines blot our voices up in their lightest sighs.
>
> Around our tent the old simplicities sough
> Sleepily as Lethe, trying to get in.
> We'll wake blank-brained as water in the dawn.

"Two Campers in Cloud Country" seems for the most part to describe the natural environment as threatening, although the description of nature as "the old simplicities" and the description of herself as "fossil" suggest even here a dissatisfaction with the separateness of the social or human world from the natural and transcendent.

"Crossing the Water" takes up this dissatisfaction more directly. The contrast here is not so much between the largeness of the landscape and the smallness of the people as between the reality of the landscape and the unreality of the people. Two "cut-paper people," they have less vitality and substance than the trees. "Where do the black trees go that drink here? / Their shadows must cover Canada." The trees have not only mobility but power.

The use of a national name implies a socially imposed boundary which to the trees is no boundary at all. The water flower leaves "are round and flat and full of dark advice." The two human intruders, who are the aliens in this setting, can become part of this world and therefore real only by becoming wordless. One of the fairy tale characters Plath implies in *The Colossus* poems is the little mermaid who, in order to be transformed, had to give up what was most precious to her, her voice. And so her tongue was cut out. This loss of a voice, obviously a crucial metaphor for a poet, can be seen in Plath's poetry in two ways. It is something that might be done to her, and as such is an expression of powerlessness. At the same time, it is something she could choose as the price for her transformation, a risk she could take to reach a reality outside her own sphere, outside of language.

In "Crossing the Water" Plath seems to be proposing a mystical experience, a union with the transcendent in the form of nature. To merge with nature, she implies, one must sacrifice the essence of society—linguistic capacity—and therefore, in a sense, die. The tradition of crossing water as a transition from life to death, from the known to the unknown, but also as a prelude to rebirth, suggests that the silence so achieved would not really be death. "As language points to its own transcendence in silence, silence points to its own transcendence—to a speech beyond silence," writes Susan Sontag.[8] While Sontag is concerned in "The Aesthetics of Silence" with the avant-garde and self-conscious cult of silence in contemporary art, of which Sylvia Plath was not knowingly a part, what she says nevertheless illuminates Plath's attitude toward language. "Behind the appeals for silence," writes Sontag,

lies the wish for a perceptual and cultural clean slate. And, in its most hortatory and ambitious version, the advocacy of silence expresses a mythic project of total liberation. What's envisaged is nothing less than the liberation of the artist from himself, of art from the particular artwork, of art from history, of spirit from matter, of the mind from its perceptual and intellectual limitations.[9]

In contrast to the liberation of silence implied in "Crossing the Water," Sylvia Plath's description of her social language-using self as fossil in "Two Campers in Cloud Country" is suggestive of inflexibility, rigidity, encrustation. A fossil is, by definition, something that was once alive, but is now dead and has been for a long time. Not even the bones are left, only an impression in stone. How does an individual interact with her world? The most immediate level is direct experience through the body, the senses. The second is through sensual language. Even farther removed from experience is abstract and intellected language. And finally, a long way off from direct experience, is linguistic self-consciousness, an awareness of the abstract nature of language. Discernible throughout Sylvia Plath's poetry is a concern with words and wordlessness, with what language is to her as a human being, as a woman, and as a poet. Her implicit suggestion in "Crossing the Water" that we give up language is an attempt to free the individual from successive encrusted layers of abstractions and to go back to direct contact with the world. Sontag suggests that:

When one talks less, one begins feeling more fully one's physical presence in a given space. Silence undermines "bad speech," by which I mean dissociated speech—speech dissociated from the body (and therefore, from feeling), speech not organically informed by the sensuous presence and concrete particularity of the speaker and by the individual occasion for using language. Unmoored from the body, speech deteriorates.[10]

For a poet who is also a woman, there is a further consideration. The inflexibility and rigidity of language hides a code of sexual/social differentiation which defines her existence in a way felt to be false. To eschew language is to provide an occasion, at the least, for existing unencumbered with what she is not. What distinguishes Sylvia Plath from other American writers—from Emerson to Pound—who have, explicitly or implicitly, proposed tearing down a tradition they have seen as outworn and encrusted and dangerous, is that she does not suggest building up again an edifice more pleasing to a new ruling class, as Genet does in *The Balcony*, where the revolutionaries became in time parodies of their former masters. To effect real change, one must explore further, dig deeper. In *Ideology and Utopia*, Karl Mannheim writes:

The world of external objects and of psychic experiences appears to be in a continuous flux. Verbs are more adequate symbols for this situation than nouns. The fact that we give names to things which are in flux implies inevitably a certain stabilization oriented along the lines of collective activity. The derivation of our meanings emphasizes and stabilizes that aspect of things which is relevant to activity and covers up, in the interest of collective action, the perpetually fluid process underlying all things. It excludes other configurational organizations of the data which tend in different directions. Every concept represents a sort of taboo against other possible sources of meaning—simplifying and unifying the manifoldness of life for the sake of action.[11]

We use language, naming, to limit our perception and to provide a stability of perception so that we can act. But if one is looking for a new way of perceiving, so that one can act and be in a new way, then it might be seen as necessary, though admittedly dangerous and perhaps impossible, to look behind our linguistic code to the actual and continuous flux of experience. Recent work by French feminist philosophers has focused on the creative and revolutionary potential of silence.

I think "feminine literature" is an organic, translated writing . . . translated from blackness, from darkness. . . . When I write there is something inside me that stops functioning, something that becomes silent. I let something take over inside me that probably flows from femininity. But everything shuts off—the analytic way of thinking, thinking inculcated by college, studies, reading, experience. . . . It's as if I were returning to a wild country. (Marguerite Duras)[12]

Writing . . . meant erasing as I went along all that had been inscribed on the slate. (Madeleine Gagnon)[13]

"The spirit of blackness is in us," Plath writes in "Crossing the Water," and if we yield, then "Stars open among the lilies. / Are you not blinded by such expressionless sirens? / This is the silence of astounded souls."

If to catalog, that is, to label, is the essence of the process of abstraction, if it demonstrates on the most primitive level the workings of a need to control the world through naming, then even Walt Whitman, thought of as the sensual voice of American poetry, is squarely in the rationalist tradition of those catalogers, beginning with Homer and the patriarchs who put the Bible together and continuing through Defoe—*Robinson Crusoe* is the greatest sustained bourgeois catalog—to Ben Franklin, the initially ragged heroes of Horatio Alger, and F. Scott Fitzgerald's Jay Gatsby, all indefatigable makers of lists. Susan Sontag suggests that the

narrative principle of the catalogue or inventory seems almost to parody the capitalist world-view, in which the environment is atomized into "items" (a category embracing things and persons, works of art and natural organisms), and in which every item is a commodity—that is, a discrete, portable object.[14]

This Apollonian need for order and control and its manifestation in a society both capitalist and patriarchal is personified in "The Surgeon at 2 A.M." (1961). One of Plath's few poems with a male persona, the surgeon shares with the snakecharmer and the sculptor (*The Colossus*) not only a need to manipulate and thereby control his environment but a formidable success in doing so. The surgeon in this poem sees people as objects—to be worked upon, perfected, put under his control, created anew. The patient has no individuality, partly because drugged: "The scalded sheet is a snowfield, frozen and peaceful. / The body under it is in my hands. / As usual there is no face." This is the other side of Plath's recurrent self-imagery of stone and hospital patient: "I have no face, I have wanted to efface myself" ("Tulips"). The individual who remains passive and indifferent will be worked on and shaped by someone else.

In "Two Campers in Cloud Country" the tension is between the human being and a real natural environment, and in "Crossing the Water" the human spirit, or yearning for the transcendent, is identified with the natural environment in opposition to language and the social individual. Plath moves one step further in "The Surgeon at 2 A.M." Here the human body as well as spirit is identified with nature and the surgeon, as an agent of "civilization," stands on the other side. The movement in the poem is from the human body as natural object to the body as historical object (marble artifact) to modern plastic object. The drugged patient is seen by the surgeon not as a whole person or even as a whole body, but in parts: "an arm or a leg, / A set of teeth or stones / To rattle in a bottle and take home." Lévi-Strauss's definition of art in *The Savage Mind* is helpful in explaining the surgeon's character.

To understand a real object in its totality we always tend to work from its parts. The resistance it offers us is overcome by dividing it. Reduction in scale reverses this situation. Being smaller, the object as a whole seems less formidable. By being quantitatively diminished, it seems to us qualitatively simplified. More exactly, this quantitative transposition extends and diversifies our power over a homologue of the thing, and by means of it the latter can be grasped, assessed and apprehended at a glance. A child's doll is no longer an enemy, a rival or even an interlocutor.[15]

Lévi-Strauss's suggestion, that the aesthetic satisfaction we derive from a work of art is proportional to how well it reduces reality to a level where we feel that we have contained and controlled something larger and more mysterious, is mirrored in the surgeon's attitude toward the human body. He begins by seeing the body as a garden, "a mat of roots," "a purple wilderness," and moves to saying

> How I admire the Romans—
> Aqueducts, the Baths of Caracalla, the eagle nose!
> The body is a Roman thing.
> It has shut its mouth on the stone pill of repose.
>
> It is a statue the orderlies are wheeling off.
> I have perfected it.

"Tomorrow the patient will have a clean, pink plastic limb," says the surgeon complacently. In this poem and through the character of the surgeon, Plath traces the course of man's progressive reduction of the world to something fragmented, artificial, and easily graspable. Certainly the surgeon is pleased with his work. The selection of Rome to stand for human history is ominous and the surgeon's admiration of Roman engineering works and the imperialistic mentality that produced them ties him to other male figures in poems like "Man in Black" and "Daddy" and to the men the secretary images in the verse play, *Three Women*. That there is a connection between these figures and an Apollonian mode of perception is suggested in the last lines of this poem: "I am the sun, in my white coat, / Gray faces, shuttered by drugs, follow me like flowers."

In moving from the human body and spirit—and society—in opposition to nature ("Two Campers in Cloud Country") to the human body and society in opposition to the human spirit aligned with nature ("Crossing the Water") and finally to a vision in "The Surgeon at 2 A.M." of the human body and spirit as well as nature all in opposition to the forces and agents of a Roman-defined (materialistic, imperialistic) society, Plath makes a statement about the progressive alienation of the individual from society which in some ways parallels R. D. Laing's description of schizophrenia in *The Divided Self*.[16] The surgeon, who personifies the modern social vision, sees human beings as objects, and whether natural, marble, or plastic, they exist fragmented and denied their individuality. People are depersonalized, in the active sense of the word, and become confused with, and no more important than, other objects that clutter up our field of perception.

It is, in this context, appropriate that in *The Bell Jar* the beginning of Esther Greenwood's breakdown is signaled by her despair over the senior thesis she is supposed to write on *Finnegan's Wake* and by her parallel perception of the landscape on her train ride home from New York: "Like a colossal junkyard, the swamps and back lots of Connecticut flashed past, one broken-down fragment bearing no relation to another" (p. 92). Plath's poems are socio-psychological in her use of her own personal situation as a model, an analogue, and a taking off point for horrors socially and historically based. This flattening out of value as people and objects become disconnected fragments begins to emerge as one of Plath's major themes in a number of the transitional poems.

"An Appearance" (1962) is about the confusion between people and the objects that surround them, a logical consequence of the ideology Plath has personified in "The Surgeon at 2 A.M." The speaker of "An Appearance," herself a curiously abstract figure, lives in a world of iceboxes, adding machines, washers, sewing machines, a television set: a reified home and clerical landscape particularly familiar to women. Love is found not in other people, but in the smile of an icebox—"Such blue currents in the veins of my loved one!"—or in the working of a sewing machine: "Is this love then, this red material / Issuing from the steel needle that flies so blindingly?" The speaker of the poem and the world she lives in reflect each other; and as the machines take on the functions of people, become more personalized, the speaker of the poem becomes depersonalized and takes on the characteristics of the machines which form her world. "What am I to make of these contradictions? / I wear white cuffs, I bow." The white cuffs suggest also the uniform of the office worker who is as much an adjunct of the machine as the factory worker and the housewife, and they remind us of the character of the Secretary in *Three Women*, written in March 1962, a month earlier than "An Appearance."

Depersonalization is also central to "Insomniac" (1961), where the imaged world is not just the speaker's immediate and personal world. The insomniac of this poem, like the persona of "Suicide Off Egg Rock," (*The Colossus*) is cursed with too much awareness. He can never shut it off into the "no-life" of sleep. Like Esther Greenwood in *The Bell Jar*, who wanted to die, but who wouldn't go to sleep, the insomniac finds that with constant awareness, things merge, flatten out, and ultimately have no meaning.

> His head is a little interior of gray mirrors.
> Each gesture flees immediately down an alley
> Of diminishing perspectives, and its significance
> Drains like water out the hole at the far end.

The images in this poem, like those in "An Appearance," come from the social world of artifacts. The black sky is carbon paper, the insomniac's "memories jostle each other for face-room like obsolete film stars," pills no longer do anything for him, outside is a "granite yard" where all night "invisible cats / Have been howling like women, or damaged instruments." What lurks behind all things is "a bonewhite light, like death." "Insomniac" ends in a description of the early morning city, where "everywhere people, eyes mica-silver and blank, / Are riding to work in rows, as if recently brainwashed." The last two lines of the poem offer an alternative to the unceasing and ultimately unproductive awareness of the insomniac. That is, one can, like the blank-eyed people riding to work in rows, be nonaware yet still physically functioning. Instead of a desert of sleeplessness and irritation, one can give in to a waking sleep, be literally brainwashed. But this is an alternative Plath obviously rejects; even the insomniac's relentless mental clamor is preferable to the death in life of the brainwashed populace. The speaker of Plath's early poems often wants to sink into a "soft caul of forgetfulness," ("Flute Notes from a Reedy Pond") but at the same time, in so doing, to transcend the waking world. As Plath's images turn from natural to social, her modes of possible escape become more limited. Where is there to get to? The death in life of those who sleepwalk through life is not an alternative she can accept.

The sense of being trapped in an increasingly narrow social and personal space and the impossibility of turning off the awareness of her entrapment—which would at least allow for a measure of complacency, if not happiness—merge in "A Life" (1960). Two levels of existence are posited in the poem, both enclosed, like the controlling metaphor of Plath's novel *The Bell Jar*, in glass. Her memory, or past life, is imaged as a glass egg and is comparable to the image of herself as an empty museum in "Barren Woman." Her present self-image is as a "foetus in a bottle," an image of suffocation also central to the novel: "to the person in the bell jar, blank and stopped as a dead baby, the world itself is a bad dream" (p. 193). The first four stanzas of "A Life" describe the scene inside the glass egg of memory. Although its inhabitants are "permanently busy," the scene is both static and unreal, as well as isolated. When she goes on to say ironically that "This family / Of valentine-faces might please a collector: / They ring true, like good china," we are back in "the country on a nursery plate" of "Watercolor of Grantchester Meadows," which she had also rejected as illusion.

The main device of "A Life," as in "Watercolor of Grantchester Meadows" and "Insomniac," is the contrast between the static, manifestly unreal picture everyone else seems to accept as reality, "like good china," and what the poet herself sees to be true, an entirely different scene. "Elsewhere the landscape is more frank." Cursed with too much awareness for comfort, like the insomniac who "lives without privacy in a lidless room," the speaker of "A Life," presumably a patient in a mental institution, finds that "the light falls without letup, blindingly."

A woman is dragging her shadow in a circle
About a bald, hospital saucer.
It resembles the moon, or a sheet of blank paper
And appears to have suffered a sort of private blitzkrieg.
She lives quietly

With no attachments, like a foetus in a bottle,
The obsolete house, the sea, flattened to a picture
She has one too many dimensions to enter.

The extra dimension is both her consciousness and her self-consciousness.

For the moment, the woman seems to live inside that bottle with grief and anger exorcised, probably by shock treatments. But Plath's attitude toward this state is clear in *The Bell Jar*, in the characterization of Valerie, Esther's co-patient in the asylum.

"Do you know what these scars are?" Valerie persisted.
"No. What are they?"
"I've had a lobotomy."
I looked at Valerie in awe, appreciating for the first time her perpetual marble calm. "How do you feel?"
"Fine. I'm not angry any more. Before, I was always angry. I was in Wymark, before, and now I'm in Caplan. I can go to town, now, or shopping or to a movie, along with a nurse."
"What will you do when you get out?"
"Oh, I'm not leaving," Valerie laughed. "I like it here" (pp. 157–58).

Not lobotomized, but increasingly angry and terrified at the narrowed horizons of her world, Plath concludes "A Life":

The future is a grey seagull
Tattling in its cat-voice of departure, departure.
Age and terror, like nurses, attend her,
And a drowned man, complaining of the great cold,
Crawls up out of the sea.

Much of the tension which informs Sylvia Plath's poetry comes from this dilemma: while she does recognize that she is inextricably entangled in her social matrix, and entangled in her society's definition of her, she never finally accepts that definition, but continues to struggle against it in her poetry, though with a growing sense of frustration. This disparity between the recognition and the acceptance of limitation is perhaps the basis both for the ambiguity of her vision and the increasingly surrealistic quality of her images. Speaking formally rather than contentually, realism can be seen as an affirmation of the values of a given society and surrealism as a refusal to accept conventional vision. From some time in late 1960 on, Sylvia Plath began increasingly to image her world as made up of walls—she does so literally in "Apprehensions" (1962)—and herself, in reflection, as fossilized. Her search for a viable redefinition of self comes up against the rigidity of social expectations codified in language and produces images of suffocation and entrapment, as well as shooting arrows and the stake finally driven into Daddy's heart. Julia Kristeva remarks: "In women's writing, language seems to be seen from a foreign land. . . . Estranged from language, women are visionaries, dancers who suffer as they speak."[17]

NOTES

1. Is *Crossing the Water* really a transitional volume, as Ted Hughes says in the prefatory note to that volume? Marjorie Perloff, in "On the Road to Ariel: The 'Transitional' Poetry of Sylvia Plath," (*Iowa Review* 4 [Spring 1973], p. 95) points out that almost half the poems in *Crossing the Water* belong to the period of *The Colossus* and that others are contemporaneous with some of the *Ariel* poems. The British editions of *The Colossus*, *Crossing the Water*, and *Winter Trees* (1971) contain different poems than the American editions of those same books. "An Appearance," "Event," and "Apprehensions," for example, appear in the Faber and Faber edition of *Crossing the Water*, but are omitted in the Harper and Row edition, and appear instead in the American edition of *Winter Trees*. The question is in one sense not important, as all the volumes after *The Colossus* are both miscellaneous and arbitrary, since the poet herself had no hand in the selection. *Crossing the Water* is not a transitional volume in the sense of forming a discrete stage in Sylvia Plath's own conception of her development as a poet, as *Life Studies*, say, does for Robert Lowell. *The Collected Poems*, ed. Ted Hughes (New York: Harper and Row, 1981), finally places all the poems in chronological order. Yet it does still seem useful to talk about a transitional period in Plath's poetry, even if that period is not identical with a particular volume of poems.

2. See the discussion of animistic projection in Sylvia Plath's poetry in Marjorie Perloff, *The Poetic Art of Robert Lowell* (Ithaca: Cornell University Press, 1973), p. 183. Also see Chapter 4, "Landscapes and Bodyscapes" in Jon Rosenblatt, *Sylvia Plath: The Poetry of Initiation.*

3. Ellen Moers, *Literary Women* (New York: Doubleday, 1976). See Chapter 5, "Female Gothic," pp. 90–99.

4. Sylvia Plath, *The Bell Jar*, p. 58. Further citations in this chapter occur in the text.

5. W. B. Yeats, *The Collected Poems of W. B. Yeats* (New York: Macmillan, 1933).

6. Margaret Dickie Uroff, *Sylvia Plath and Ted Hughes*, p. 76.

7. Lois Ames, "Notes Toward a Biography," pp. 171–72.

8. Susan Sontag, "The Aesthetics of Silence," in *Styles of Radical Will* (New York: Farrar, Straus and Giroux, 1966), p. 18.

9. Ibid., pp. 17–18.

10. Ibid., p. 20.

11. Karl Mannheim, *Ideology and Utopia* (New York: Harcourt, Brace and World, 1936), p. 22.

12. Marguerite Duras, "From an Interview" in Elaine Marks and Isabelle de Courtivron, eds., *New French Feminisms* (New York: Schocken, 1980), p. 174.

13. Madelaine Gagnon, "Body I" in Elaine Marks and Isabelle de Courtivron, eds., *New French Feminisms* (New York: Schocken, 1980), p. 179.

14. Sontag, p. 26.

15. Claude Lévi-Strauss, *The Savage Mind* (Chicago: University of Chicago Press, 1966), pp. 23–24.

16. Laing, *The Divided Self.* See especially Chapters 4 and 5: "The Embodied and Unembodied Self" and "The Inner Self in the Schizoid Condition."

17. Julia Kristeva, "Oscillation Between Power and Denial" in Marks and de Courtivron, eds., *New French Feminisms*, p. 166.

❧ 4 ❧

Three Women: "I Shall Be a Heroine of the Peripheral"

Considering the vast range of poems on death and mortality, it is surprising that such a fundamental experience as birth has so little literature of its own—until, of course, one remembers how few great poets have themselves been mothers.

Douglas Cleverdon, producer
of *Three Women* for the BBC[1]

The center of Sylvia Plath's art is a tension between words and wordlessness, stasis and movement, entrapment and potentiality. Her one dramatic piece, *Three Women*, a radio play in verse written for the BBC in spring of 1962, explores this tension through its focus on a crisis situation uniquely female, the act of giving birth. The setting is a maternity ward. The play alternates between three monologues: the First Voice is the Wife, who gives birth to and keeps her child, the Second Voice is the Secretary, who miscarries, and the Third Voice is the Girl, who has her child and leaves it. Grouped around an apparently straightforward biological act are complicated questions of communication, creativity, and the nature of the relation between an individual woman and her society. Finally, *Three Women* is about what stands in the way of creativity—biological and aesthetic—in a bureaucratized society that confuses the word with the thing, the signifier with what is signified, and in a capitalist society that alienates the producer from what is produced, including babies, and commoditizes most products, including poems.

Plath remarked in a letter to her mother (June 7, 1962): "I've had a long poem (about 378 lines!) for three voices accepted by the BBC Third Programme (three women in a maternity ward, inspired by a Bergman film)."[2] *Three Women* is based on one of Ingmar Bergman's less known films, *Nära Livet* (*The Brink of Life* or *So Close to Life*), made in 1957 and first shown in March of 1958.[3] Bergman's film also centers on three women in the maternity ward of a hospital, and though Plath borrowed this basic structure, she made a number of significant changes in characterization and in form. In *The Brink of Life*, the three women are Cecilia, a secretary who miscarries in her third month; Stina, a 25-year-old factory worker who is married and wants her child, only to have it born dead; and Hjördis, a 19-year-old factory worker who is not married, does not want her child and comes to the hospital for an abortion; however, as a result of her interactions with the other two women she decides to have the child instead. Hjördis's situation corresponds to that of the Third Voice, the Girl, in Plath's play. Cecilia corresponds to the Second Voice, the Secretary, and Stina is most like Plath's First Voice, the Wife. Bergman himself based his film on a short story, "The Aunt of Death," by Ulla Isaksson, who wrote the screenplay for the film. Bergman and Isaksson in their collaboration changed the original story by adding the third character, Hjördis.

In Bergman's film, the experience of the three characters is generally negative: a miscarriage, a stillbirth, and a possible abortion. The film does end on a positive note, however, in Hjördis's decision to have her child. Plath probably initially was attracted to the film in the light of her own recent experiences. In the previous two years, she had had a miscarriage (February 6, 1961), as well as giving birth to her two children in 1960 and 1962.[4] She changes substantially the situations of Stina and Hjördis, who become her First and Third Voices. The Wife in Plath's play does not have a stillborn child, but a normal, live boy. In fact, her experience becomes emblematic of the normal experience of marriage, childbirth, and motherhood, and thus provides as wide a contrast as possible to the situation of the Second Voice, the Secretary. In

The Brink of Life[5] and in *Three Women* as well, the Secretary's experience is central, her voice the closest to the voice we hear in Plath's greatest poems. Hjördis, the young woman who becomes Plath's third voice, is distinguished in Bergman's film by being the only character who develops and changes. In Plath's play, in contrast, the Girl is the most static of the three characters. She has her child, a daughter, and leaves it; there is no suggestion that she has considered any other alternative.

   The Brink of Life is one of the most documentary of Bergman's films.

In keeping with his striving for an ascetic approach, Bergman uses no flashbacks, no dream sequences, no expressionistic photography, and his actresses wear no makeup. The setting throughout the entire film is the naked, antiseptic hospital milieu, and most of the action is confined to one room.[6]

Bergman "wanted the style to be as bare as possible" in order to concentrate on the inner lives of his characters. In many ways, *Three Women* retains this starkness of style, though the rich imagery of the poetry somewhat softens the bareness of the situation. Plath, using a verbal rather than a visual medium, can take us immediately to the inner lives of her three women, or at least to what Plath chooses to have them tell us about their inner lives.

   Perhaps the most significant change in Plath's adaptation of *The Brink of Life* is the play's structure of three intercut monologues. Peter Cowie, in his critical biography of Bergman, remarks about the film: "The women sense a need to huddle together emotionally. They are stripped of their pretensions and purged of their bitterness by *mutual* suffering. . . . 'Not only our wombs open here, but our entire being,' comments Cecilia"[7] (italics mine). It is, for example, through Hjördis's interaction with the other two women in Bergman's film that she finally changes. Plath's three women, in contrast, are deliberately and formally isolated from each other throughout the play. Also, in Bergman's film there are other characters: hospital personnel and, most crucially, the three men, whose attitude toward pregnancy and childbirth and toward the women who are bearing their children significantly affects the three women. In Plath's play no other characters speak: only the

three women—the Wife, the Secretary, the Girl—each locked into
her own experience. Failure to communicate and the lack of potential for change through some relation to others is, then, not
only a theme but a formal element in the play. As audience, we
hear now one, now another, of the three voices, but they do not
hear and consequently cannot respond to each other.

The failure of communication within the formal structure of the
play is an important aspect of Sylvia Plath's developing image of
the world and herself as woman and as poet in relation to it. In
making pregnancy and birth the center of her play, Plath brings
us back to the literal question of the possibility of creativity in an
alienated world. The "specific content" of *Three Women* is the isolation of each of these women inside her own experience and,
more crucially, inside the social definitions of that experience.[8]
The form of the play, three intercut monologues, is a direct reflection of its content.

Recurring throughout the speeches of the Wife, the Secretary,
and the Girl is a concern with the perception and definition of
"normality." The self-image of each of the three women in Plath's
play is in large part founded upon how near (or distant) she feels
from the postwar American definition of woman as mother. Betty
Friedan writes in 1963 in *The Feminine Mystique* that:

stories in women's magazines insist that woman can know fulfillment
only at the moment of giving birth to a child. They deny the years when
she can no longer look forward to giving birth, even if she repeats that
act over and over again. In the feminine mystique, there is no other way
for a woman to dream of creation or of the future. There is no other way
she can even dream about herself, except as her children's mother, her
husband's wife.[9]

It is the very tension or opposition between an individual and his
environment that determines the development as well as the
expression of his personality suggests George Lukács in "The Ideology of Modernism."[10] In such poems as "The Applicant" in
Ariel and in the characterization of the Secretary, the Second Voice
of *Three Women*, Plath grapples most directly with the numbing
effect of a bureaucratized society upon the creative potential of the
individual. She juxtaposes pregnancy and childbirth on the one

hand, and the failure to produce children on the other hand, with this attitude toward motherhood as the sole means of fulfillment for a woman. In *Three Women*, she carefully distinguishes between the actual experience of giving birth and the social definition of that experience.

Plath's ambivalent attitude in this play toward the experience of giving birth is expressed in part by her setting, the maternity ward of a hospital. In her own experience, the hospital was never associated with birth, but with sickness, madness, and death. The hospital imagery of Plath's late poems almost always stands for impersonality, depersonalization, loss of control of one's own body, sterility, and flatness. Between 1951 and 1962, she developed the hospital, the office, and the concentration camp as her major metaphors for contemporary society. In a letter written during her undergraduate years she had described "ecstatically" a visit to Boston Lying-in Hospital.

I spent the whole night there—going around from room to room with the older medical students and doctors. . . . I stood two feet away to watch a baby born, and I had the queerest urge to laugh and cry when I saw the little squinted blue face grimacing out of the woman's vagina— only to see it squawk into life, cold, naked and wailing a few minutes later. . . . Needless to say, my sense of the dramatic was aroused, and I went skipping excitedly down the corridors of the maternity ward like a thoroughly irresponsible Florence Nightingale.[11]

By 1961–62, when she was writing *The Bell Jar* and *Three Women*, Plath recorded this experience very differently. In the novel, Esther Greenwood tells of a visit to a maternity ward with Buddy Willard, a medical student she is dating.

I was so struck by the sight of the table where they were lifting the woman I didn't say a word. It looked like some awful torture table, with these metal stirrups sticking up in mid-air at one end and all sorts of instruments and wires and tubes I couldn't make out properly at the other. . . .

Later Buddy told me the woman was on a drug that would make her forget she'd had any pain and that when she swore and groaned she really didn't know what she was doing because she was in a kind of twilight sleep.

I thought it sounded just like the sort of drug a man would invent. Here was a woman in terrible pain, obviously feeling every bit of it or she wouldn't groan like that, and she would go straight home and start another baby, because the drug would make her forget how bad the pain had been, when all the time, in some secret part of her, that long, blind, doorless and windowless corridor of pain was waiting to open up and shut her in again.[12]

What repels Esther Greenwood about this experience is not only the pain of giving birth, but also the numbing effect produced by the drugs the woman has been given. She is cut off from her own labor, performing it unconsciously. The *non*-alienated labor of the delivery room is performed by men; the woman has no conscious part in her own act of childbirth. Birth ritual and child-rearing practices are usually a good index to the ideology of a given culture, and in *Thinking About Women*, Mary Ellman remarks that:

Childbirth itself, in the United States, is so locked in the concept of male "attendence" or "delivery" as to seem paralytic. They disappear, these women, wrapped in sheets and wheeled on carts, like (the other) mummies. It is the doctor who emerges, upright, calm, flecked with blood: "It's a boy."[13]

Lois Ames, in "Notes Toward a Biography," relates a story about Sylvia Plath's own birth. When Sylvia was born on October 27, 1932, her father, Otto Plath, announced:

"All I want from life from now on is a son born two and a half years to the day." Mrs. Plath obligingly brought forth Warren Joseph on April 27, 1935. Professor Plath's colleagues toasted him as "the man who gets what he wants when he wants it."[14]

Partly because she was living in England at the time, neither of Sylvia Plath's own two children was born in a hospital. Douglas Cleverdon, producer of *Three Women* for the BBC, writes:

My wife recalls the enthusiasm with which Sylvia Plath talked about the birth of her two children—the first in a London flat in a somewhat seedy square near Primrose Hill, with a sweet and gentle Indian girl as midwife;

the second in a Devonshire village, where the local midwife was also one of the beekeepers whose rituals are celebrated in "The Bee Meeting."[15]

Plath's own experience with childbirth, then, involved neither hospitals nor male attendence. Her one experience with pregnancy and hospitals consists of her miscarriage in 1961; this experience parallels that of the Secretary, the Second Voice of *Three Women*.

Fertility and sterility are recurring motifs in Sylvia Plath's poetry. Dionysus and Apollo, the transcendent and the rational, the sensual and the abstract, roundness and flatness, are set off against each other. The speaking sensibility of Plath's poems often sees herself as part of the rational, intellected, Apollonian world and identifies this with the daily reality of contemporary, bureaucratic Western culture. The other world, which the speaker of the poems yearns toward, is Dionysian, wordless, sensual, where there remains a possibility of mystical union with what exists beyond and before the social. That Sylvia Plath chose to make the setting of most of this play a maternity ward, with all the connotations that hospitals already had for her, suggests that *Three Women* is not merely a hymn to creativity through childbirth. While Plath is celebrating the act of giving birth, she is at the same time pointing out contemporary conditions that encroach even upon this possibility for transcending self and returning to a wordless state of oneness with the universe. All three of the women in this play are, in varying degrees, trapped within the definitions of creativity which their society has assigned to them.

There has been little critical attention to *Three Women*, and what there is has tended to see the First Voice as the center of the play.[16] Certainly the Wife, who bears her child and keeps it, has a more normal experience than either the Girl, who gives her child away, or the Secretary, who cannot bear a child at all. But it is precisely this normality which highlights in contrast the experience of the Second Voice, the Secretary, who most closely approximates Plath's image of the more likely relationship in the contemporary world between an individual and her social context. The situation of the Wife is potentially the most positive, but it is finally undercut; the last voice we hear in the play is that of the Secretary.

Two factors characterize the First Voice, the Wife. First is the experience of actually giving birth, which Plath presents as a ritual and miracle in which the universe is shattered and recreated and the individual attains for a brief moment a sense of oneness and identification with the transcendent, by focusing inward and banishing self-consciousness of her socially defined self. Second, and immediately following this mystical experience, she feels a protectiveness toward the child which seems to be derived from fear. This fear and possessiveness grow through the Wife's last four speeches until they fill every corner of her world and redefine her image of herself and her world in a socially engendered and alienating way.

In her first speech, which is also the opening speech of the play, the Wife is turned inward, away from her social context. Tensely calm, she waits in anticipation of a portentous and mysterious event, a mood similar to part of "Poem for a Birthday" (*The Colossus*), written when Plath was pregnant with her first child, Frieda. But even in her opening speech, complacency characterizes this First Voice: "I am slow as the world. I am very patient, / Turning through my time, the suns and stars / Regarding me with attention."[17] Throughout this first speech, she is the center of the universe in tune with time and with the natural world of which she feels herself a part. "Leaves and petals attend me. I am ready," she says.

Her second and third speeches are of labor, in a productive, non-alienated sense. "I last it out. I accomplish a work," she says. Here, as in the earlier "Poem for a Birthday," the birth of the child is seen as an occasion, at least potentially, for the woman's death and rebirth; she images herself as "a seed about to break," as Mary cloaked in blue, as a shell on a beach waiting for the tide. The images in these speeches are destructive as well as unitive, and the power she feels within herself is both centralizing and fragmenting: "A power is growing on me, an old tenacity. / I am breaking apart like the world." Finally, at the moment of birth, she loses consciousness: "I see nothing."

The motif of protectiveness begins in the Wife's third speech; it is a protectiveness based in part on a sense of ownership and a corresponding fear of loss. "I shall be a wall and a roof," she says in her third speech, and "I shall not let go" in her fourth. She fears the separation she feels between herself and this child which has been part of her body. By her sixth speech, the extent of this protectiveness is clear when she asks: "How long can I be a wall around my green property?"

If we have come to sympathize and identify with the Wife's experience throughout the play—and certainly her experience is happier than either the Secretary's or the Girl's—we nevertheless begin to feel uneasy during the Wife's seventh and last speech, for it is no longer a record of a mystical and unifying experience, but merely a paean of praise to normality. At home again, she is reminded by the flowers and birds of the seasons and of the cycle of time: "I hear the sound of the hours / Widen and die in the hedgerows." She says, "I am reassured" and "I shall meditate upon normality." Specifically, she contrasts her child to those born deformed:

> I do not believe in those terrible children
> Who injure my sleep with their white eyes, their fingerless hands.
> They are not mine. They do not belong to me.
>
> I shall meditate upon normality.
> I shall meditate upon my little son.

Sylvia Plath herself was concerned enough about birth defects to write a poem called "Thalidomide," to go to the 1960 Ban the Bomb protest in England, and to write in a letter to her mother, "Already a certain percentage of unborn children are doomed by fallout."[18] However, by the Wife's seventh speech "normality" has begun to take on sinister and stifling connotations. Foreshadowed by the complacency of her first speech, the Wife's last speech is smug. It reminds us of the political climate of postwar America Sylvia Plath had grown up in, with its slogan "a return to normalcy"—which also meant a return to isolation and a willed blindness to horrors that exist outside one's safe, enclosed world, as well as a resolute lack of sympathy shading into paranoid terror of anything not normal. It reminds us of the fear projected into science fiction films of the 1950s with titles like *The Thing*, *It*, and *Invasion of the Body Snatchers*. The Wife's attitude in her last speech parallels the attitude of an America during the decade after the Second World War that sent money to war ravaged Europe and Japan but that did not want to think too closely about the victims of concentration camps and atomic bombs. And within this play, the Wife's attitude will begin to strike us as selfish and ungenerous in the context of the situation of the Secretary, who is unable to give birth to a child at all.

The imagery of both self and world in the Wife's last speech echoes some of Sylvia Plath's earlier poems, particularly "Watercolor of Grantchester Meadows" in *The Colossus* and "A Life" and "The Surgeon at 2 A.M." in *Crossing the Water*. In "Watercolor of Grantchester Meadows," the benign surface of a scene described as "a country on a nursery plate" is smashed in the last stanza as an owl swoops down to seize a mouse. In "A Life," Plath similarly contrasts a glass egg world "where the sea waves bow in single file. / Never trespassing in bad temper" to another place, where "the landscape is more frank" and "the light falls without letup, blindingly." Plath had, clearly and fairly early, rejected as naive, self-deceptive, and unreal the view that either art or life is a stilled and tranquil perfection. However, Plath assigns to the Wife in her last speech the same imagery that she herself earlier had rejected as dangerously illusive:

> I am reassured. I am reassured.
> These are the clear bright colors of the nursery,
> The talking ducks, the happy lambs.
> I am simple again. I believe in miracles.

The Wife also echoes the words of the surgeon in "The Surgeon at 2 A.M.," who says about his postoperative patient: "It is a statue the orderlies are wheeling off. / I have perfected it. . . . Tomorrow the patient will have a clean, pink plastic limb." Describing, perhaps by this time even gloating over, her son, the Wife says in her final speech: "But he is pink and perfect."

By the end of the play, then, the Wife has become a possessive, self-deceiving stereotype of motherhood. Yet the actual experience of giving birth that she is the center of is meant to be experienced by the audience as a celebration. As the Wife moes away from this experience of transcendence and back into her social milieu, she seems to be moving into a world that is less powerful, less secure, and, oddly enough, less real. While Plath points out the possibilities for both realizing and transcending self in the act of creation, she also points out, through the Wife's own unself-conscious description of herself in relation to her child, the limitations and dangers in the contemporary social definition of motherhood.

The Girl who is a student, the Third Voice of *Three Women*, is in some ways the least complicated of the three characters. She is also the least important, formally; she has only six speeches, 12 stanzas, and eighty-four lines in the play, far fewer lines than either the Wife or the Secretary. (The Wife has seven speeches, 19 stanzas, 133 lines; the Secretary has seven speeches, 22 stanzas, 154 lines.) And the Girl's experience is bracketed within those of the Wife, who opens the play, and the Secretary, who closes it. She is the most static character in the play. "I wasn't ready" is the key phrase in the Girl's first speech; this contrasts with the Wife's repeated statement, "I am ready." The discovery the Girl's pregnancy forces her to is that acts do have consequences; now she sees "every little word hooked to every little word, and act to act." The Girl uses this image of hooks over and over and, for her, hooks always imply unwelcome responsibilities. She does not wish to be responsible; she wants to be removed from the cycle of nature, as did the girl in Plath's poem "Spinster" (*The Colossus*) who, confronted with an unruly and sensuous springtime, "withdrew neatly." Here, the Girl does not have that particular choice: "I thought I could deny the consequence— / But it was too late for that." However, within the range of choice left to her, she does withdraw neatly: She has the child and leaves it.

There is an abstractness in this Third Voice, this student, which is not in the speeches of either the Wife or the Secretary. Perhaps because of her refusal to be committed to anything, she is less tied to the sensual world. Because she is a student, and because she chooses that role over motherhood, she is on the side of rationality, intellect, much more so than the Secretary, whose sterility is not a matter of choice. In a letter written in late 1956 or early 1957 while she was married and a student at Cambridge, Sylvia Plath had referred to herself as a "triple-threat woman: wife, writer & teacher (to be swapped later for motherhood, I hope)."[19] This desire to be all three, to be everything, to "shoot off in all directions myself, like the colored arrows from a Fourth of July rocket,"[20] which in *The Bell Jar* becomes a paralzying conflict between fulfilling one's potentiality on the one hand and a heavy conditioning toward home and children on the other hand, may account for the ambivalence in tone which characterizes *Three Women* and particularly Plath's harsh description of the student, with whom Plath herself might feel some identification.

Plath allows selfishness to permeate the speeches of the Third Voice. While allusions to Narcissus are made in the speeches of both the Wife and the Girl, it is only in the Wife's final speech that she says, "the narcissi open white faces in the orchard." In contrast, the Girl's opening speech describes her looking at herself in a pool.

> I remember the minute when I knew for sure.
> The willows were chilling,
> The face in the pool was beautiful, but not mine—
> It has a consequential look, like everything else.

The Wife's selfishness includes and is in part founded on one other, her child, while the Girl's includes only herself. She is physically self-conscious and consistently describes herself from the outside. Even in our introduction to her, we are allowed first to see her only through her reflection in a pool. In her second speech, in the maternity ward, she again describes herself in terms of the way she looks to others. "I am a mountain now, among mountainy women. / The doctors move among us as if our big-ness / Frightened the mind."

For the Girl, unlike the other two women, giving birth is solely a physical experience. At the time it is not part of her identity because finally neither commitment nor consequences are involved. Plath, therefore, does not give us an account of the Girl's labor but moves directly to a description of her reactions to her new child. The Girl's third speech is contrasted to the Wife's fourth and fifth speeches, between which it appears. The Wife's child, who is wanted and loved, is male, while the Girl's child, un-wanted and rejected, is female. And while the Wife sees her rela-tionship to her new son as protective and loving, the Girl sees her daughter as a threat: alien, frightening, and dangerous. The two passages parallel and contrast in imagery and movement; one is a negative of the other. The Wife ends by saying: "I shall not let go. / There is no guile or warp in him. May he keep so." The Girl concludes her third speech thus: "My daughter has no teeth. Her mouth is wide. / It utters such dark sounds it cannot be good." The issues again is perception of normality. The Wife has to believe in her son's normality for it is the most important point to her, while the Girl sees her daughter as alien and odd-looking even though she is, presumably, physically normal.

The Girl's fourth speech shows her leaving the hospital and the child she has rejected: "I undo her fingers like bandages." Her next speech is some time later, at her graduation, and again we are given a description of her surface: "My black gown is a little funeral: / It shows I am serious." Here also is a confirmation of her rejection of and distance from the experience of childbirth: "It was a dream, and did not mean a thing." The Girl's sixth and last speech loops back to her first. Again she is in the meadow near the river. "The swans are gone," she says, those swans that heralded for her a kind of divine birth. All births, for Plath, are in some way sacred. The Girl's pregnancy is given pagan connotations, as the Wife's, in her image of herself as Mary, is given Christian connotations. But now the swans are gone and the Girl feels a vague sense of loss. In her opening speech she had deplored "every little word hooked to every little word, and act to act." In her last speech she congratulates herself: "It is so beautiful to have no attachments! / I am solitary as grass." She has now what she wanted—no attachments, no responsibilities, no hooks—but in contrast to her first speech, where she twice said, "I wasn't ready," here she repeats and ends with: "What is it I miss?"

In the Girl's last speech and throughout the Secretary's speeches, we sense their guilt at having deviated from the expected role of motherhood. Friedan writes about the fifties:

In those ten years the image of American woman seems to have suffered a schizophrenic split.

The new feminine morality story is the exorcising of the forbidden career dream, the heroine's victory over Mephistopheles: the devil, first in the form of a career woman, who threatens to take away the heroine's husband or child, and finally, the devil inside the heroine herself, the dream of independence, the discontent of spirit, and even the feeling of a separate identity that must be exorcised to win or keep the love of husband and child.[21]

The guilt that characterizes the Girl's last words in *Three Women* is present from the very beginning of the Secretary's speeches. She is unable to bear a child at all and as a result, defines herself as not normal, "neither man nor woman," a freak. This guilty doubt of her own womanliness is also true of Cecilia in Bergman's *The Brink of Life*, who "complains that her baby 'flowed from me to serve some scientific experiment.' "[22] The Secretary has an awareness of her self, her world, and the conflict between self and world that the other two voices in the play lack. The Secretary has more lines than either of the other two speakers and she has the last word; her seventh speech ends the play. The world she lives in, like the world imaged in much of Sylvia Plath's poetry at this period, is closed, static, and sterile.

The transformations and sense of potentiality of *The Colossus* poems have diminished by the time Sylvia Plath writes *Three Women*. Although there is still in this play a possibility of a transcendence of the social world in the emotional and physical experience of giving birth, personified here in the Wife, even this experience cannot be sustained; it melts away when the self returns to her social context. The speaker of Plath's poems from 1959 on is trapped within her society, or at least the borders have become more rigid. The colors of the post-*Colossus* poems are increasingly harsh and sharp-edged as the world of the poems becomes more rigid, flat, and drained of possibility. The colors now are stark black and white, with splotches of crimson in poems like "Tulips."[23] Bright colors are threatening but real—the Nazi flag is black, white, and red; pastels or soft harmonious colors or nursery colors signify a landscape (as in "A Life," "The Disquieting Muses," and in the Wife's last speech in this play) which we are to see as self-deluding and unreal.

The colors of the Secretary's world are black and white and red: typewriter keys, hospital sheets, unanswered letters, the barren moon, lipstick, and blood:

> When I first saw it, the small red seep, I did not believe it.
> I watched the men walk about me in the office. They were so flat!
> There was something about them like cardboard, and now I had
>   caught it,
> That flat, flat, flatness from which ideas, destructions,

Bulldozers, guillotines, white chambers of shrieks proceed,
Endlessly proceed—and the cold angels, the abstractions.

The ambivalent and uncomfortable relationship between self and world in the Secretary's speeches is characteristic of Plath's late poems. The Secretary's first words connect and oppose the world of bureaucracy (the office where she works) to her own pregnancy, the social to the biological. In contrast, the First Voice and the Third Voice are alone. Plath makes a similar connection between bureaucracy and sterility in "The Applicant" (*Ariel*), where relations between men and women are equated with the personnel office matching of employer and employee. In both "The Applicant" and *Three Women*, a world of mechanized and frustrated labor corresponds to a world of mechanized and frustrated love, sexuality, and reproduction. A bureaucratized society will vitiate both the relation of one person to another and of a person to his or her work. The two will be mirror images. What the Secretary has caught from the flat world, from the men in the office, is some quality like cardboard which symbolically and really causes in some way her recurrent miscarriages. This paper imagery occurs often in the *Ariel* poems ("Lady Lazarus," "Cut," "The Applicant") and suggests that the self so described lacks substance, depth, and color; that is, reality. As in Theodore Roethke's 1948 poem about office work, "Dolor," people are two-dimensional in a world of three-dimensional artifacts.

The Secretary in *Three Women* lives in a world of men and machines, and has begun to take on those qualities of flatness, abstractness, rationality, and rigidity which Plath has, in the post-*Colossus* poems, consistently seen as directly inimical to sensuality, transcendence, roundness, and the possibility of change and creativity. In this first speech, the Secretary directly images herself as an extension of a machine.

The letters proceed from these black keys, and these black keys
   proceed
From my alphabetical fingers, ordering parts,

Parts, bits, cogs, the shining multiples.
I am dying as I sit. I lose a dimension.

The most often repeated word in the Secretary's first speech is "death." As the birth of her child is for the Wife also a rebirth for herself, so here the death of the child is a kind of death for the Secretary as well. Her imagery is of bare trees, empty sky, and herself with no relation even to a barren nature. Instead: "These are my feet, these mechanical echoes. / Tap, tap, tap, steel pegs." If the Wife is described in Christian imagery and the Girl in pagan imagery, then the imagery of the Secretary and her world is first from modern technology and second from the grimmer of Grimm's fairy tales and the folklore from which those tales derive.

The emptiness which characterizes the Secretary's self-image and which was metaphorized as barren nature in her first speech becomes in her second specifically the faces of her unborn children. She is in the hospital now, and her sense of emptiness and flatness is directly contrasted to the succeeding speech of the Wife, who sees herself as "a seed about to break." Unlike the sightless, inward focused gaze of the Wife, the Secretary, like the speaker of "Insomniac" in *Crossing the Water*, cannot turn off her vision. And she sees not only the bald, unfeatured faces of her dead and unborn children, but also sees "other faces. The faces of nations, / Governments, parliaments, societies, / The faceless faces of important men." What follow are the bitter but perceptive lines suggesting that her own inability to be a "normal" woman is directly related to the flatness of the male world she lives in and has to some extent accepted. She is an integer in it, an integral part of it. She has partaken of their flatness. She is like them.

> It is these men I mind:
> They are so jealous of anything that is not flat! They are jealous
>   gods
> That would have the whole world flat because they are.
> I see the Father conversing with the Son.
> Such flatness cannot but be holy.
> "Let us make a heaven," they say.
> "Let us flatten and launder the grossness from these souls."

The third and fourth speeches of the Secretary, juxtaposed to the reactions of the Wife to her son and the Girl to her daughter, are about the Secretary's own self-image in relation to a barren earth and moon. Her third speech is characterized by images of blood and bloated passion. "I dream of massacres. / I am a garden of black and red agonies." The Secretary's speeches constantly move back and forth between her own situation and the society outside of yet still mirroring her own inability to create. The world loves death and sees in death its goal. "It is a love of death that sickens everything. / A dead sun stains the newsprint. It is red." The earth is like the witch in "Hansel and Gretel": "So she supports us, / Fattens us, is kind. Her mouth is red." Finally, the earth is "the vampire of us all," an image that often appears in the *Ariel* poems ("Lady Lazarus," "Mary's Song," "Daddy"). In the bureaucratic world Plath envisions in her late poems, the individual is papery, unreal, empty, and dead. Horror is oral. People are characterized by a kind of psychic hunger. We are dead and eat the world (or the world eats us, it hardly seems to matter) in order to make it as dead as ourselves. And victim becomes victimizer, for according to the legend, once consumed by a vampire one becomes in turn vampire and so the cycle goes on. Sylvia Plath's vampire imagery is for the individual what her World War II imagery, with its impersonal massacres and its concentration camps, is for society. Often one shades into the other, as in "Daddy," where the central figure is both vampire and gestapo officer.

The connection between the situation of the individual woman and the society she lives in is also clear in the Secretary's fourth speech. Here the moon is a connecting link between her own self-image and her image of her world. Like the moon, the Secretary sees herself as barren, pale, and empty; she is forced to start over again each month and each beginning leads nowhere. She identifies herself as well with what the moon shines on because they are all empty: "that chalk light / Laying its scales on the windows, the windows of empty offices, / Empty schoolrooms, empty churches." All of these—offices, schoolrooms, churches—are of course metaphors for social ordering: business and government, formal education, and organized religion.

The Secretary· is the only one of the three women concerned with and self-conscious about her identity, largely because she is unsure about it. (The Third Voice is also self-conscious but seems to know who she is.) The Secretary does not fit the social definition of woman as mother, and so she says, "I see myself as a shadow, neither man nor woman." She is the only one of the three who ultimately, and unsatisfactorily, has to find her identity in more abstract social terms: "The nurses give back my clothes, and an identity." Even her situation, she finds, is not unique, does not possess a tragic singularity. "I am not hopeless," she says. "I am beautiful as a statistic." Her clothes, the lipstick she puts on, her job (the fact that she has one and therefore has to be at a certain place at a certain time) are what give her her identity. She is so much a part of the well-oiled nine-to-five machinery that even her personal crises occur on weekends. "I can go to work today," she says, and function "a little sightless," "on wheels, instead of legs," "speak with fingers, not a tongue." As in "The Applicant," Plath uses metonymy here to describe the woman not only as a collection of parts (literally fragmented) but as parts which are artifacts.

In her last speech, which is also the last speech of the play, the Secretary is at home with her husband, being a wife. She says twice that she feels she is healing and that she feels a tenderness both in nature (the spring air) and in the human world (the lamp-light). And certainly the last words of the play are hopeful: "The city waits and aches. The little grasses / Crack through stone, and they are green with life." But even within this last speech, an explicit statement of warmth and hope, her own activity is activity leading nowhere.

> My hands
> Can stitch lace neatly on to this material. My husband
> Can turn and turn the pages of a book.
> And so we are at home together, after hours.
> It is only time that weighs upon our hands.

What distinguishes the Second Voice of *Three Women* from the other two speakers is not only her inability to create biologically but also through most of the play her tragic self-awareness, her consciousness of the conflict between her creative needs and the world she lives in. The other two women are in some measure blind in their narcissism. The Girl is blind in her selfishness and in her refusal to connect acts to consequences. The Wife, in her need to protect and possess her child, wants to believe in a nurs-ery-plate vision of normality, where motivations are benign and proportions harmonious. But the Secretary, in her desire to have children and in her inability to have any, is forced toward sight. Further, she is the only one of the three women who is a worker and who therefore participates in the reality of alienated work. She is the only one of the three women whose world is imaged consistently in the harsh and blindingly stark colors which char-acterize Sylvia Plath's late poems. She is the only one who is aware of the hostility in purpose between her biological and personal goals and the goals of the larger society she lives in.[24] And yet she also sees herself as part of this world which is finally inimical to her creativity. She is fatally involved in it. Her "flaw," which makes her the tragic center of this play and which distinguishes her from the Wife and the Girl, is her at least partial rejection of illusion based on her knowledge that she is inextricably a part of the world she lives in.

What then of the last lines of the play which seem to indicate a blindness that is hope and a desire to return to a normality she has earlier defined as illusory? Perhaps it is a hope that contains an awarenenss of all that has happened. Or perhaps the ending of *Three Women*, like the forced gaiety of *The Bell Jar*'s ending, is a problem in the play, since it seems to contradict the world that has been presented throughout the work. Or perhaps, in spite of what Esther Greenwood has been through and now knows and in spite of what the Secretary knows, they continue to hope in order to continue to live. Moreover, the Secretary's last speech, in which she sews lace while her husband flips through the pages of a book, is undercut by her fourth and pivotal speech, in which she tells us "It is over" (the miscarriage) and works out a plan for her life which will at least keep her going.

> I shall be a heroine of the peripheral.
> I shall not be accused by isolate buttons,
> Holes in the heels of socks, the white mute faces
> Of unanswered letters, coffined in a letter case.
> I shall not be accused, I shall not be accused.
> The clock shall not find me wanting, nor these stars
> That rivet in place abyss after abyss.

The ambivalence with which *Three Women* ends is a prelude to many of the poems collected in *Ariel*, which move beyond ambivalence to a bitter satire that uses the socially based and worldwide horrors of World War II as a structure of imagery to define her own personal situation. Here in *Three Women* Plath seems to be still working out what the nature of the society she lives in is and what the possibilities are for coming to terms with this necessary involvement of the individual woman in her society. Her conclusions are not optimistic. The experience of birth should be the Dionysian transcendence of self and merging with self which the Wife alone among the three women experiences, but even she loses this when she returns to her socially defined self. Mid-twentieth-century corporate bureaucracy undercuts the creative possibilities of the self. The Secretary's world is this social world, bureaucratic, machine-dominated, populated by cardboard people who seem finally not quite as real as the artifacts that surround them. In such a world, real and sustained creativity is difficult. All three women survive by choosing blindness in varying degrees, from the Wife's almost total retreat into a nursery world of illusion through the Girl's abdication of responsibility to the Secretary's conscious decision to be numb. What *Three Women* finally says is that one can no longer be a heroine of the central and the real, merely a heroine of the peripheral.

NOTES

1. Douglas Cleverdon, "On *Three Women*" in *The Art of Sylvia Plath*, p. 228. Plath sent Cleverdon the script of *Three Women* early in May 1962. It was produced and recorded on August 2 for the Third Programme and broadcast on September 13.

2. Aurelia Schober Plath, ed., *Letters Home, by Sylvia Plath* (New York: Harper and Row, 1975), p. 456.

3. Filmography, from Peter Cowie, *Ingmar Bergman: A Critical Biography* (New York: Charles Scribner's Sons, 1982), p. 372.
NÄRA LIVET (*Brink of Life* or *So Close to Life*) 1958

Screenplay: IB, Ulla Isaksson, based on the short story, "Det vänliga, várdiga," in her book *Dödens faster*. Photography: Max Wilén. Art Direction: Bibi Lindström. Medical Adviser: Dr. Lars Engström. Editing: Carl-Olov Skeppstedt. Production Company: Nordisk Tonefilm. 2,310 meters. 84 minutes. Swedish premiere: March 31, 1958.

Cast: Eva Dahlbeck (Stina Andersson), Ingrid Thulin (Cecilia Ellius), Bibi Andersson (Hjördis), Barbro Hiort af Ornäs (Sister Brita), Erland Josephson (Anders Ellius), Inga Landgré (Greta Ellius), Max von Sydow (Harry Andersson), Gunnar Sjöberg (Dr. Nordlander), Anne-Marie Gyllenspetz (welfare worker), Sissi Kaiser (Sister Marit), Margareta Krook (Dr. Larsson), Lars Lind (Dr. Thylenius), Monica Ekberg (Hjördis's friend), Gun Jonsson (night nurse), Inga Gill (woman), Gunnar Nielsen (a doctor), Maud Elfsiö (trainee nurse), Kristina Adolphson (assistant).

4. *Letters Home*, p. 408.
5. John Donner, *The Personal Vision of Ingmar Bergman*, trans. Holger Lundbergh (Freeport, N.Y.: Books for Libraries Press, 1964), pp. 21–24. Though Donner, like a number of other Bergman critics, sees *Brink of Life* as one of Bergman's more disappointing films, he remarks the conversation between Cecilia and her husband, a typical Bergman intellectual, as one of the most powerful scenes in the film.
6. Birgitta Steene, *Ingmar Bergman* (New York: Twayne Publishers, 1968), p. 58.
7. Cowie, *Ingmar Bergman: A Critical Biography*, p. 170.
8. Lukács. "The Ideology of Modernism," p. 19.
9. Friedan, *The Feminine Mystique*, p. 55.
10. Lukács, "The Ideology of Modernism," p. 28.
11. Quoted in Lois Ames, "Notes Toward a Biography," in *The Art of Sylvia Plath*, p. 161.
12. Sylvia Plath, *The Bell Jar*, p. 53.
13. Mary Ellman, *Thinking About Women* (New York: Harcourt Brace Jovanovich, 1968), p. 79.
14. Ames, "Notes Toward a Biography," p. 156.
15. Cleverdon, "On Three Women," in *The Art of Sylvia Plath*, p. 228.
16. For example, in Eileen Aird's short study, *Sylvia Plath: Her Life and Work* (New York: Harper & Row, 1973):

> The Wife's experience is pivotal; that of the Girl and the Secretary being implicitly compared and contrasted with it. . . . Sylvia Plath explores in 'Three Women' the subject of creativity as it is revealed in three separate situations and it is on the Wife's central experience that she dwells in the greatest detail (p. 53).

Jon Rosenblatt, in *Sylvia Plath: The Poetry of Initiation*, remarks that the Wife's experience is "normative" and locates in her monologue the rebirth symbolism that is his central concern (p. 115).
17. Sylvia Plath, *Three Women* in *The Collected Poems of Sylvia Plath*,

Three Women first appeared in *Winter Trees* (New York: Harper & Row, 1972).

18. *Letters Home*, p. 378.
19. Ames, "Notes Toward a Biography," p. 166.
20. Plath, *The Bell Jar*, p. 68.
21. Friedan, *The Feminine Mystique*, p. 40.
22. Cowie, *Ingmar Bergman: A Critical Biography*, p. 170.
23.

> Against the whiteness of the hospital, the white sheets, the white cold wing of the great swan, the white clouds rearing, a world of snow, there is projected "a garden of black and red agonies." The Wife, "center of an atrocity," gives birth to "this blue, furious boy," the Girl to "my red, terrible girl"; beneath the moon that "drags the blood-black sea around, month by month," the Secretary is bled white as wax. The evocation of vivid colour is matched in intensity by the startling directness of the imagery; and the emotional experience is shaped by poetic discipline into the most austere and monosyllabic forms. In radio, nothing can equal a poet's visualizing imagination, dramatically expressed in clear and speakable language.

Cleverdon, "On *Three Women*," p. 229.

24. Plath revises Bergman's personal representation of this issue to a social level. Birgitta Steene writes in her study of Bergman:

> The three fathers [in *Brink of Life*] are responsible for the women's attitude toward childbirth. Stina's husband is a solid, down-to-earth man whose uncomplicated nature stands in direct relation to Stina's joyful expectancy. Ellius, Cecilia's husband, is a Bergman intellectual, a nihilistic type that frequently is to play the role of devil archetype and succeeds the earlier father-tyrant figure in Bergman's films. Ellius does not wish to have children, which has created a neurotic attitude in Cecilia toward the baby she has been expecting. She blames herself for its loss, but Bergman suggests that Cecilia may have desired its death for fear of her husband's resentment of the child.
>   The father of Hjördis' child does not appear. His denial of responsibility leads Hjördis to reject the thought of a baby."

Steene, *Ingmar Bergman*, p. 59.

✌ 5 ✌

A Disturbance in Mirrors:
The Late Poems

Marked by a conflict between stasis and movement, isolation and engagement, Sylvia Plath's late poems are largely about what stands in the way of the possibility of rebirth for the self. In "Totem," she writes:

> There is no terminus, only suitcases
>
> Out of which the same self unfolds like a suit
> Bald and shiny, with pockets of wishes,
>
> Notions and tickets, short circuits and folding mirrors

While in the early poems the self was often imaged in terms of its own possibilities for transformation, in the post-*Colossus* poems the self is more often seen as trapped within a closed cycle. One moves, but only in a circle and continuously back to the same starting point. Rather than the self and the world, the *Ariel* poems record the self in the world. The self can change and develop, transform and be reborn, only if the world in which it exists does; the possibilities of the self are intimately and inextricably tied to those of the world. The poems locate meaning in the dialectical tension between images of self and images of world.

This perceptual change in Sylvia Plath's poetry of the relationship between self and world parallels the development of a number of other postwar American poets whose subject has increasingly become an examination of the connections and the conflicts between self and world. In the poetry of so-called confessional poets Anne Sexton and Robert Lowell, the focus is more on the self as the world impinges upon it.[1] For other contemporaries of Plath's, those who lived on to develop into the political poets of the late 1960s and the 1970s, anti–Vietnam war and feminist poets like Denise Levertov, Muriel Rukeyser, and Adrienne Rich, the focus has been as much on analysis of the context in which the aware self exists as it is a description of the self that world daily implodes into.

For Plath, the antinomies latent in the *Colossus* poems become central and explicit in the later poetry: stasis or unceasing and meaningless movement, the mind opaque to the rest of the world or controlled by an awareness which can never be turned off, isolation and a sense of suffocation or a painfully acute vulnerability and a fear of too much room, the sense that the world is entirely a subjective landscape and the equally strong sense that that landscape and especially we as part of it exist depersonalized or as dismembered fragments, as assertion of self in the definite and very personal voice Plath develops in the poetry from 1960 on at the same time that these poems are a prelude to silence and the dissolution of that voice. The self moves and is still, is isolated and engaged, alternatively and simultaneously. Whether there is any end result to movement in the context of these antinomies and, given this question, what kind of movement is possible, is finally the subject of the *Ariel* poems and many of the poems originally collected in *Winter Trees*.[2]

In Sylvia Plath's early poems, the world is imaged for the most part in natural terms; it is static, cyclic, nonhuman, and immortal. The relation of the self to this world is in terms of its own possibilities for change and transformation. In *The Colossus*, the world does not move, the self does. After *The Colossus*, however, Plath increasingly images the world as a social and contemporary landscape: an an office, a battlefield or concentration camp, a kitchen, a hospital. Natural images continue to appear in these late poems, as social images occasionally appeared in the early poems, but these natural images—the elm tree, the moon, the beehive—though they have a mythic dimension, exist within the context of a social and socialized world. The earlier poems had employed images directly from a variety of mythologies, and Judith Kroll shows Plath's familiarity with the work of Graves, Neumann, and Jung, among others.[3] What Plath does in her late poems is to create her own system of mythology based on modern historical images and events, a mythology whose central figure is a protean female protagonist, hero, victim, goddess.

One might think that the knowledge that the self exists in the world rather than parallel to it would lead to greater freedom and to an enlarged sense of possibility. At least it would give one a practical reference point for action and imagination. However, its initial result, in the literature of marginalized groups, is instead often a greater sense of constriction and entrapment.[4] If, as an American woman writing in the 1950s and early 1960s, your initial perception of the relationship between self and society is that the possibilities are truly limited, then where do you go from such knowledge? A repeated question in the *Ariel* poems is simply that: Where is there to get to?

The tension between stasis and movement, isolation and engagement, and the preoccupation with a resolution of this tension through rebirth, are central to one of Plath's greatest poems, "Tulips" (March 18, 1961). The conflict between hanging on and letting go, between rebirth and death, placed in a hospital setting, is background for not only "Tulips," but also "Paralytic" (January 29, 1963), "In Plaster" (March 18, 1961), the verse play *Three Women* (March 1962), and "The Stones" (November 4, 1959) in *The Colossus*, which most commentators on Plath's poetry see as the first appearance of the voice of the late poems. The central image in "Paralytic" and "In Plaster" is the physical confinement of the individual within a cast, literally unable to move. In the early poem, "The Stones," the speaker of the poem is a stone in "the city where men are mended" (based on a folktale with the same title in Paul Radin's *African Folktales and African Sculpture*). As a stone and passive, various things are done to her, parts are replaced, until at the end of the poem she can say, though we don't necessarily believe it, "I shall be good as new." "Tulips" is like "The Stones" in its movement of the speaker of the poem toward renewal, but there is a crucial difference. In "The Stones" the speaker of the poem, in her self-image as stone, is completely passive; all that is done is done *to* her. In "Tulips," in contrast, where there is the same conflict between passivity, peace, and abdication of responsibility on the one hand and passion and activity on the other hand, the conflict takes place within the speaker of the poem rather than outside. In "The Stones" the only action the speaker of the poem takes is to "cry out" so that she can be found. After that, she does not need to do anything; the process of renewal and rebirth is quite automatic. In "Tulips," however, the speaker of the poem must decide for herself whether she wants to come back. She must make a choice between the world of the hospital and the white passivity it represents and the world of the tulips with its red, agitating life. The stone imagery of the earlier poem is in part retained, but where in "The Stones" the self *is* a stone, here the self is like a stone to others. "My body is a pebble to them, they tend it as water / Tends to the pebbles it must run over, smoothing them gently. / They bring me numbness in their bright needles, they bring me sleep." The choice, then, is located within the self. The self must act within the world rather than in some mythical and metaphorical realm outside the world.

The two realms between which the speaker of the poem must choose are represented by the hospital and by the tulips. In various manifestations, these are also the two poles of the *Ariel* poems as a whole. The hospital is associated in "Tulips" with winter and its reduced life functions of dormancy, hibernation, and endurance; with water; with coldness; with numbness and sleep; with emptiness and flatness; with neutrality, a state of null emotions; with detachment, sterility, depersonalization, purification, and peacefulness. The hospital represents a peeling off of encumbrances, a kind of return to an essential, blank state. "I am nobody," says the speaker of the poem, echoing Emily Dickinson. "And I have no face, I have wanted to efface myself." "I have given my name and my day-clothes up to the nurses / And my history to the anaesthetist and my body to surgeons." Later in the poem she reasserts this as she watches her tea-set, her bureaus of linens, and her books sink into the water a moment before she herself goes under. Finally, what the hospital represents is a fading away of the self, an escape from the cycle of death and rebirth at its lowest ebb.

How free it is, you have no idea how free—
The peacefulness is so big it dazes you,
And it asks nothing, a name tag, a few trinkets.
It is what the dead close on, finally; I imagine them
Shutting their mouths on it, like a Communion tablet.

The world of the hospital is the present world of the speaker of the poem and the rhythm of the poem corresponds to this lassitude, this drugged, slow-motion state. The lines are long, Whitmanic, with series like "as the light lies on these white walls, this bed, these hands." However, while Whitman's long breath line was meant to signify a kind of cosmic inclusiveness, Plath's naming of things in "Tulips" is for the opposite purpose. As she names them, they disappear, as though the word cancels out the thing in a kind of reverse incantation, until finally everything will have been named, and there will be nothing left, and the world will be pure and clean and blank. Working from the most superficial associations down to the most essential, she can blank things out one by one, until only she is left, and she can say Sylvia, and she too will disappear.

This is one alternative inherent in the *Ariel* poems and, in a literal sense, it is the alternative that Sylvia Plath herself finally chooses. Not without a struggle, however; and it is the struggle, rather than the final choice, that forms both the emotional tension of the poems and their interest for the reader. "Tulips" itself is so structured that it is clear from the first line of the poem that the speaker's choice will be life. "The tulips are too excitable, it is winter here." The first four of the poem's nine stanzas describe the world of the hospital in the yearning tones of one who has already turned her back on it and knows it is slipping away. By the fifth and pivotal stanza, she is already referring to her wish to remain in the hospital world in the past tense: "I didn't want any flowers, I only wanted / To lie with my hands turned up and be utterly empty." The last four stanzas of the poem describe the tulips and their effect on her, which is painful in the way one's arm feels when it has fallen asleep and the circulation has started to return. The tulips represent color as opposed to the pallidness and whiteness of the hospital; they represent warmth in contrast to the chill of the hospital, passion in contrast to peace, noise in contrast to silence, the organic in contrast to the inorganic, self-consciousness in contrast to the loss of self the hospital offers.

> Nobody watched me before, now I am watched.
> The tulips turn to me, and the window behind me
> Where once a day the light slowly widens and slowly thins,
> And I see myself, flat, ridiculous, a cut-paper shadow
> Between the eye of the sun and the eyes of the tulips.

When she describes the tulips in terms of their color and weight, as "a dozen red lead sinkers round my neck," the long euphonious line of the poem becomes, with its monosyllabic words, more compact and jarring.

This description of the tulips as lead sinkers which will finally pull her under the water to drown suggests the central ambivalence in the *Ariel* poems, for her relation to the world of the hospital is also described in terms of drowning. To accept the world of the tulips with its attendant baggage of "loving associations"—"my husband and child smiling out of the family photo"—is to surrender the self to social expectations and institutions. "Tulips" suggests that underneath an apparent set of opposites there is really no difference and no choice, that one will drown no matter which alternative one chooses.

Nevertheless, one must still choose: between the alternatives one is given or new alternatives one structures oneself. Sylvia Plath's late poetry is at least implicitly political in Lukaĉ's terms, in which "a character's conception of the world represents a profound personal experience and the most distinctive expression of his inner life; at the same time it provides a significant reflection of the general problems of his time."[5] Sylvia Plath's sense of entrapment, her sense that her choices are profoundly limited, is a direct reflection of the particular time and place in which she wrote her poetry. Betty Friedan, whose book *The Feminine Mystique* (1963) is particularly helpful in understanding the world Plath was writing out of, describes the late 1950s and early 1960s for American women as a "comfortable concentration camp—physically luxurious, mentally oppressive and impoverished."[6] Suffocating in her home under a junkheap of consumer goods, the world beyond the home a gigantic supermarket, radio advertisements and billboards informing her of needs she hadn't even got around to articulating yet, the individual woman who thought poems were more important than possessions was already in trouble.[7] That Plath herself frequently and gleefully in her letters to her mother listed her publications and how much cash they had brought in that year suggests the extent to which even a woman critical of a product and "thing" oriented society is affected by its basic assumptions.[8] From inside a concentration camp, comfortable or not, it is difficult to structure new alternatives.

The attempt to find new alternatives still exists, however, in that the late poems are not merely lyrical outcries but explore a dynamic relationship between self and world. In an otherwise profoundly misleading and patronizing foreword to the American edition of *Ariel*, Robert Lowell nevertheless makes one good point when he describes the poetic voice of the *Ariel* poems as a character and the poems as a whole in terms of plot. This conception of Plath's poetic self-image as a character and the *Ariel* poems as a narrative, connected by a consistency of language, is, I think, accurate. She builds up a picture of a world for us and of herself in various guises moving through it, worrying at it, trying to find in the chaos a comfortable balance, some ground on which to stand.

The way in which Sylvia Plath is a character with many faces in her poems, the way the consistency of her self-image nevertheless operates within the poems in the same way character does in a narrative is perhaps best illustrated by contrasting Plath's poetic self-image with that of Ted Hughes, with whom she lived from June 16, 1956, when they married, until they separated some time during the summer of 1962.[9] While Plath frequently describes herself as a victim in her poems, Hughes consistently in his poems takes on the persona of a predator. Much of the central subject matter of both these poets is, first, the relationship between man and woman and the possibility of love. Second, and closely connected to the first, their subject is the quality of the relationship between the individual and external events. How much control does the individual have over her or his life? What are the possibilities of change—of the individual changing her or himself, of the individual changing the world? Both Plath and Hughes characterize the world as a chaotic, brutal, and dehumanizing place. Plath often sees the conditions of her world as so overpowering that she cannot hope to change them and must struggle merely to retain her self and to attempt to grow within conditions so inimical to growth that she feels she must continually start over again. Thus, Lady Lazarus, who says, "I have done it again," and who continually finds herself back in the same place, looking at the same amused faces.

In contrast, the personae of Hughes's poems—an otter, a fox, a rat, a wolf, a pike, a crow—are in relative control of their world. Sometimes, as in "Ghost Crabs" (*Wodwo*), they are personifications of the chaos that lurks outside our ordered and unreal social world. Sometimes, as in many of the poems in *Crow*, the perspective of the poem is that of the predator, so alien to human values that he confounds even God, a hesitant liberal with whom Crow is often seen in conversation. Crow represents the harsh indifferent real world that for Hughes exists behind our hopeful and illusory explanations. In "Crow's First Lesson," God tries to teach Crow to say "Love." Instead, Crow retches, "And woman's vulva dropped over man's neck and tightened." The two fight, God struggles to part them and Crow flies away. This conception of the violence inherent in relationships between men and women is characteristic of Hughes's poems. "The Lovepet" (*Crow*) describes love as a stray and carnivorous animal the man and woman have found and adopted and that, insatiable, devours them piece by piece. "It ate their future complete."

Even when the personae of Hughes's poems are human and not some metaphorical predatory animal, the relation between man and woman often is brutalized. In "Her Husband" (*Wodwo*), the central character is a coal miner who comes home at night determined to make his wife suffer as he feels he has suffered. "Let her learn," he says, and "he'll humble her."[10]

Mary Ellman wrote that "poets may choose now to play either penitent or priest, but no one wants to be prime minister."[11] Given our Romantic heritage, a poet might also choose to play prophet. All of these choices imply a kind of relationship between poet and subject matter, self-image and image of the world, writer and audience. It seems to me that the role Hughes chooses to play in these poems is that of priest, explaining and to some extent legitimizing a metaphysics of tooth and claw that he sees existing underneath our civilized veneer. Sylvia Plath, on the other hand, is half penitent, half prophet, unwilling to accept either the social or the metaphysical explanations she had been given, but unable to replace them, as Hughes seems to be able to, with another completed system, for to construct a paradigm implies that, for the moment at least, one is satisfied with the structure one has to work with. Instead, Plath's poetry suggests not only dissatisfaction with but powerlessness in the face of external events and man's history; the collective persona of her poems is locked between the twin mirrors of the world and her own mind.

What Sylvia Plath's poetry celebrates is movement and process. In "Years," (November 16, 1962) she writes:

> Eternity bores me,
> I never wanted it.
>
> What I love is
> The piston in motion—
> My soul dies before it.
> And the hooves of the horses,
> Their merciless churn.
>
> And you, great Stasis—
> What is so great in that!

What her poetry questions, given her perception of the limited possibilities open to her, is where there is to get to. Is one actually moving, or is one standing on a treadmill, watching the same scenery go past repeatedly? What her poetry fears is that there are only the two alternatives: an Apollonian, intellectual response to the world, which has the result of separating her from it and making her live in a paradigm instead of in reality; and a Dionysian, wordless, and cyclic response, which entails dissolution of the self into an all-embracing other. On the one hand, the self would exist cut off by intellect from all that is not self; on the other hand, the self would cease to exist at all as it is absorbed into the other. That her sense of possibility was limited is not only a significant comment on her specific historical period, a time of isolationism, subjectivity, and fear of experience, but a comment as well upon the relative freedom of men and women artists throughout much of western history. Virginia Woolf wrote in 1928:

For surely it is time that the effect of disencouragement upon the mind of the artist should be measured, as I have seen a dairy company measure the effect of ordinary milk and Grade A milk upon the body of a rat. They set two rats in cages side by side, and of the two one was furtive, timid and small, and the other was glossy, bold and big. Now what food do we feed women as artists upon?"[12]

THE SOCIAL CONTEXT

While a painfully acute sense of the depersonalization and fragmentation of 1950s America is characteristic of the late poems, three of them describe particularly well the social landscape within which the "I" of Sylvia Plath's poems is trapped: "The Applicant," "Cut," and "The Munich Mannequins."[13] The recurring metaphors of fragmentation and reification—the abstraction of the individual—in Plath's late poetry are socially and historically based. They are images of Nazi concentration camps, of "fire and bombs through the roof" ("The Applicant"), of cannons, of trains, of "wars, wars, wars" ("Daddy"). They are images of kitchens, iceboxes, adding machines, typewriters, and the depersonalization of hospitals. The sea and the moon are still central images, but in the poems from 1961 on they take on a harsher quality. "The moon, also, is merciless," Plath writes in "Elm."

One of the more bitter poems in *Ariel* is "The Applicant" (October 11, 1962), a portrait of marriage in contemporary western culture. However, the "courtship" and "wedding" in the poem seem to represent not only male/female relations but human relations in general. That the applicant also can be seen as applying for a job or buying a product suggests a close connection between the capitalist economic system, the patriarchal family structure, and the general depersonalization of human relations. Somehow all interaction between people, and especially that between men and women, given the history of the use of women as items of barter, is conditioned by the ethics and assumptions of a bureaucratized market place. However this system got started, both men and women are implicated in its perpetuation. As in many of Plath's poems, one feels in reading "The Applicant" that Plath sees herself and her imaged personae as not merely caught in—victims of—this situation, but in some sense culpable as well. In "The Applicant," the poet is speaking directly to the reader, addressed as "you" throughout. So we, too, are implicated, for we are also potential "applicants."

In the first stanza of "The Applicant," as in the beginning of "Event" (May 21, 1962), people are described as crippled and as dismembered pieces of bodies. Thus the theme of dehumanization begins the poem. Moreover, the pieces described here are not even flesh, but "a glass eye, false teeth or a crutch, / A brace or a hook, / Rubber breasts or a rubber crotch." We are already so implicated in a sterile and machine-dominated culture that we are likely part artifact and sterile ourselves. One is reminded of the "clean pink plastic limb" which the surgeon in "The Surgeon at 2 A.M." complacently attaches to his patient. One is also reminded of Chief Bromden's conviction, in Ken Kesey's *One Flew Over the Cuckoo's Nest*, written at about the same time as "The Applicant," that those people who are integrated into society are just collections of wheels and cogs, smaller replicas of a smoothly functioning larger social machine. "The ward is a factory for the Combine," Bromden thinks, "something that came all twisted different is now a functioning, adjusted component, a credit to the whole outfit and a marvel to behold. Watch him sliding across the land with a welded grin."[14]

In stanza two of "The Applicant," Plath describes the emptiness which characterizes the applicant and which is another version of the roboticized activity of Kesey's Adjusted Man. Are there "stitches to show something's missing?" she asks. The applicant's hand is empty, so she provides "a hand"

> To fill it, and willing
> To bring teacups and roll away headaches
> And do whatever you tell it.
> Will you marry it?

Throughout the poem, the people are talked about as parts and surfaces. The suit introduced in stanza four is at least as alive as the hollow man and mechanical doll woman of the poem. In fact, the suit, an artifact, has more substance and certainly more durability than the person to whom it is offered "in marriage." Ultimately, it is the suit which gives shape to the applicant where before he was shapeless, a junk heap of fragmented parts.

> I notice you are stark naked.
> How about this suit—
>
> Black and stiff, but not a bad fit.
> Will you marry it?
> It is waterproof, shatterproof, proof
> Against fire and bombs through the roof.
> Believe me, they'll bury you in it.

The man in the poem is finally defined by the black suit he puts on, but the definition of the woman shows her to be even more alienated and dehumanized. While the man is a junk heap of miscellaneous parts given shape by a suit of clothes, the woman is a windup toy, a puppet of that black suit. She doesn't even exist unless the black suit needs and wills her to.

> Will you marry it?
> It is guaranteed
>
> To thumb shut your eyes at the end
> And dissolve of sorrow.
> We make new stock from the salt.

The woman in the poem is referred to as "it." Like the man, she has no individuality, but where his suit gives him form, standing for the role he plays in a bureaucratic society, for the work he does, the only thing that gives the woman form is the institution of marriage. She does not exist before it and dissolves back into nothingness after it. There is at least the implication that something exists underneath the man's black suit; that however fragmented he is, he at least *marries* the suit and he at least has a choice. In contrast, the woman *is* the role she plays; she does not exist apart from it. "Naked as paper to start," Plath writes,

But in twenty-five years she'll be silver,
In fifty, gold.
A living doll, everywhere you look.
It can sew, it can cook,
It can talk, talk, talk.

The man, perhaps a junior-executive corporation type, is also alienated.[15] He has freedom of choice only in comparison to the much more limited situation of the woman. That is to say, he has relative freedom of choice in direct proportion to his role as a recognized worker in the economic structure of his society. This should not imply, however, that this man is in any kind of satisfying and meaningful relation to his work. The emphasis in "The Applicant" upon the man's surface, the necessity for putting on that black suit and the opening question of the poem. "First, are you our sort of person?", suggests that even his relationship to his work is not going to be in any sense direct or satisfying. It will be filtered first through the suit of clothes, then through the glass eye and rubber crotch before it can reach the real human being, assuming there is anything left of him.

The woman in the poem is seen as an appendage; she works, but she works in a realm outside socially recognized labor. She works for the man in the black suit. She is seen as making contact with the world only through the medium of the man, who is already twice removed. This buffering effect is exacerbated by the fact that the man is probably not engaged in the type of work that would allow him to feel some relationship to the product of his labor. He is probably a bureaucrat of some kind, and therefore his relationship is to various pieces of paper, representative of successive and fragmented paradigms of the product, rather than to the product itself. And of course, the more buffered the man is, the more buffered the woman is, for in one sense, her relationship to the real world of labor is that of consumer rather than producer. Therefore, her only relationship to socially acceptable production, as opposed to consumption, is through the man.

In another sense, however, the woman is not a consumer but a commodity. Certainly she is seen as a commodity in this poem, the reward the man receives, only slightly less important than the black suit, for being "our sort of person." It can be argued that the man is to some extent also a commodity; yet just as he is in one sense more a worker and less a consumer than is the woman, in terms of the social recognition of his position, so in this second sense he is more a consumer and less a commodity than the woman. And when we move out from the particularly flat, paper-like image of the woman in the poem to the consciousness which speaks the poem in a tone of bitter irony, then the situation of the woman as unrecognized worker–recognized commodity becomes clearer. The man in "The Applicant," because of the middle-class, bureaucratic nature of his work (one does not wear a black suit to work in a steel mill or to handcraft a cabinet) and because of his position vis-à-vis the woman (her social existence depends upon his recognition), is more a member of an exploiting class than one that is exploited.[16] There are at least some parts of his world, specifically that involving the woman, in which he can feel himself in relative control and therefore able to understand his relationship to his world in a static and contemplative way. Thus, whatever we may think of the system he has bought into, he himself can see it as relatively stable, a paradigm with certain static features which nevertheless allows him to move upward in an orderly and progressive fashion.

Within the context of the poem, then, and within the context of the woman's relationship to the man in the black suit, she is finally both worker and commodity while he is consumer.[17] Fredric Jameson, in *Marxism and Form*, defines the kind of perception of external objects and events which arises naturally in the consciousness of an individual who is both worker and commodity simultaneously:

even before [the worker] posits elements of the outside world as *objects* of his thought, he feels *himself* to be an object, and this initial alienation within himself takes precedence over everything else. Yet precisely in this terrible alienation lies the strength of the worker's position: his first movement is not toward knowledge of the work but toward knowledge of himself as an object, toward self-consciousness. Yet this self-consciousness, because it is initially knowledge of an object (himself, his own labor as a commodity, his life force which he is under the obligation to sell), permits him more genuine knowledge of the commodity nature of the outside world than is granted to middle-class "objectivity." For [and here Jameson quotes Georg Lukács in *The History of Class Consciousness*] "his consciousness is the self-consciousness of merchandise itself."[18]

This dual consciousness of self, the perception of self as both subject and object, is characteristic of the literature of marginalized or oppressed classes. It is characteristic of proletarian writers in their (admittedly sometimes dogmatic) perception of their own relation to a decadent past, a dispossessed present, and a utopian future. It is characteristic of black American writers. W.E.B. DuBois makes a statement very similar in substance to Jameson's in *The Souls of Black Folk*, and certainly the basic existential condition of Ellison's invisible man is his dual consciousness, which only toward the end of that novel becomes a means to freedom of action rather than paralysis.[19] It is true of contemporary women writers, such novelists as Doris Lessing, Margaret Atwood, and Maxine Hong Kingston, and of such poets as Audre Lorde, Adrienne Rich, and Marge Piercy. In some sense it is more a long-standing characteristic of American literature than of any other major world literature, for each immigrant group, however great its desire for assimilation into the American power structure, at least initially possessed this dual consciousness. Finally, a dialectical perception of self as both subject and object, as both worker and commodity, of self in relation to past and future as well as present, is characteristic of revolutionary literature, whether the revolution is primarily political or cultural.

Sylvia Plath has this dialectical awareness of self as both subject and object in particular relation to the society in which she lived. The problem for her, and this is perhaps the problem of Cold War America, is in the second aspect of a dialectical consciousness: an awareness of oneself in significant relation to past and future. The first person narrator of what is probably her best short story, "Johnny Panic and the Bible of Dreams," is a clerk/typist in a psychiatric clinic who describes herself as a "dream connoisseur," who keeps her own personal record of all dreams which pass through her office, and who longs to look at the oldest record book the Psychoanalytic Institute possesses. "This dream book was spanking new the day I was born," she says, and elsewhere makes the connection even clearer: "the clinic started thirty-three years ago—the year of my birth, oddly enough."[20] This connection suggests the way in which Plath uses history and views herself in relation to it. The landscape of her late work is a contemporary social landscape. It goes back in time to encompass such significant historical events as the Rosenberg trial and execution—around which the opening chapter of *The Bell Jar* is structured—and of course it encompasses, is perhaps obsessed with, the major historical event of her time, the Second World War. But social history, reference to actual historical events, seems to stop for Plath where her own life starts, and is replaced at that point by a mythic timeless past populated by creatures from folk tale, fairy tale and classical mythology. This is not surprising, since as a woman she had scant affirmation of her part in shaping history. Why should she feel any relation to it? But more crucially, there is in Sylvia Plath's work no imagination of the future, no utopian or even anti-utopian consciousness. There is a dialectical consciousness in her poetry of the self as simultaneously object and subject, but she was unable to develop in her particular social context a consciousness of herself in relation to a past and future beyond her own lifetime. This foreshortening of a historical consciousness affects in turn the dual consciousness of self in relation to itself (as subject) and in relation to the world (as object). It raises the question of how one accounts objectively for oneself. If I am involved in everything I see, is it still possible for me to be objective and empirical in my perception, free from assumptions inherent in culture, history, language? Finally, this foreshortening of historical consciousness affects the question of whether the subject is a function of the object or vice versa. Since the two seem of equal possibility, the question is never resolved. As a result, the individual feels trapped; and in Sylvia Plath's poetry one senses a continual struggle to be reborn into some new present; but when the perceiving consciousness opens its eyes, it discovers that it has instead, as she says in "Lady Lazarus," made a

theatrical

Comeback in broad day
To the same place, the same face, the same brute
Amused shout:

"A miracle!"

This difficulty in locating the self and the suspicion that as a result the self may be unreal are clear in poems like "Cut" (October 24, 1962) which describe the self-image of the poet as paper. The ostensible occasion of "Cut" is slicing one's finger at the kitchen counter instead of an onion; the first two stanzas of the poem describe the cut finger in minute and almost naturalistic detail. The suppressed hysteria here is only discernible in the poem's curious mixture of surrealism and objectivity. The images of the poem are predominantly images of terrorism and war, immediately suggested to the poet by the sight of her bleeding finger: "Little pilgrim, / The Indian's axed your scalp," "Out of a gap / A million soldiers run," "Saboteur / Kamikaze man—," a reference to the Ku Klux Klan, and finally, "Trepanned veteran." The metaphors of war and violence are extensive, and, though suggested by the actual experience, they are removed from it.

The one place in the poem where the speaker mentions how she herself feels, as a complete entity including her cut finger, the image is of paper. She says,

> O my
> Homunculus, I am ill.
> I have taken a pill to kill
>
> The thin
> Papery feeling.

The image of paper to describe the self-image of the poet is used consistently in the post-*Colossus* poems. It is used in the title poem of *Crossing the Water*, where the "two black cut-paper people" appear less substantial and less real than the solidity and immensity of the natural world surrounding them. In the play *Three Women*, the Secretary says of the men in her office: "There was something about them like cardboard, and now I had caught it." She sees her own infertility as directly related to her complicity in a bureaucratic, impersonal, patriarchal society. Paper is symbolic of our current socioeconomic reality with its characteristic bureaucratic paper-shuffling labor. It stands for insubstantiality; the paper model of something is clearly less real than the thing itself, though in "developed" economies it seems to be the office machines, accoutrements, and objects which have vitality, purpose, and emotion, while the people are literally colorless, objectified, and atrophied. Theodore Roethke, an important influence on Plath's poetry from 1959 on, also wrote about the deadening effect of bureaucratic institutions. In "Dolor" (1948) he describes "the inexorable sadness of pencils," "the duplicate grey standard faces," the "ritual of multigraph, paper-clip, comma, / Endless duplication of lives and objects."[21] For both Plath and Roethke, it is as Roethke writes the "dust from the walls of institutions" that is alive, while human beings seem to have faded and flattened into the walls.

The paper self is, then, part of Plath's portrait of a depersonalized society, a bureaucracy, a paper world. In "A Life" (*Crossing the Water*), she writes:

> A woman is dragging her shadow in a circle
> About a bald hospital saucer.
> It resembles the moon, or a sheet of blank paper
> And appears to have suffered a sort of private blitzkrieg.

In "Tulips" the speaker of the poem, also a hospital patient, describes herself as "flat, ridiculous, a cut-paper shadow / Between the eye of the sun and the eyes of the tulips." In "The Applicant," the woman is again described as paper: "Naked as paper to start / But in twenty-five years she'll be silver, / In fifty, gold." Here in "Cut," the "thin, / Papery feeling" juxtaposes her emotional dissociation from the wound to the realistic description of the cut and the bloody images of conflict it suggests. It stands for her sense of depersonalization, separation of self from self, and is juxtaposed to the devaluation of human life which is a necessary precondition to war, the separation of society from itself. In this context, it is significant that one would take a pill to kill a feeling of substancelessness and depersonalization. Writing about American women in the 1950s, Betty Friedan asks

Just what was the problem that had no name? What were the words women used when they tried to express it? Sometimes a woman would say, "I feel empty somehow . . . incomplete." Or she would say, "I feel as if I don't exist." Sometimes she blotted out the feeling with a tranquilizer.[22]

A papery world is a sterile world; this equation recurs through-out the poems originally collected in *Ariel*. For Sylvia Plath, stasis and perfection are associated with sterility and/or death, while fer-tility is associated with movement and process. The opening lines of "The Munich Mannequins" (January 28, 1963) introduce this equation. "Perfection is terrible," Plath writes, "it cannot have children. / Cold as snow breath, it tamps the womb / Where the yew trees blow like hydras." The setting of "The Munich Man-nequins" is a city in winter. Often, Plath's poems have imaged winter as a time of rest preceding rebirth ("Wintering", "Frog Autumn"), but only when the reference point is nature. The world of nature is characterized in her poems by process, by the ebb and flow of months and seasons, by a continual dying and rebirth. The moon is, in that context, a symbol for the monthly ebb and flow of the tides and of a woman's body. The social world, how-ever, the world of the city, is both male-defined and separated from this process. In the city, winter has more sinister connota-tions; it suggests death rather than hibernation. Here the cold is equated with the perfection and sterility to which the poem's opening lines refer. Perfection stands in "The Munich Manne-quins" for something artificially created and part of the social world.

The poem follows man's quest for perfection to its logical end— mannequins in a store window—lifeless, and mindless "in their sulphur loveliness, in their smiles." The description of the man-nequins is contrasted to the real woman in the same way that the city is contrasted to the moon. The real woman is not static but complicated:

> The tree of life and the tree of life
>
> Unloosing their moons, month after month, to no purpose.
> The blood flood is the flood of love,
>
> The absolute sacrifice.

However, in Munich, "morgue between Paris and Rome," the artificial has somehow triumphed. Women have become manne-quins, have been replaced by mannequins, or at least mannequins are seen to have a greater reality because they are more ordered and comprehensible than real women.

It is appropriate that Plath should focus on the middle class of a German city, in a country where Fascism was a middle-class movement and women allowed themselves to be idealized, to be "perfected," to be made, essentially, into mannequins. In "The Munich Mannequins," as in "The Applicant," Plath points out the deadening of human beings, their disappearance, fragmentation and accretion into the objects that surround them. In "The Applicant" the woman is a paper doll; here she has been replaced by a store-window dummy. In "The Applicant" all that is left of her at the end is a kind of saline solution; in "The Munich Mannequins" the only remaining sign of her presence is "the domesticity of these windows, / The baby lace, the green-leaved confectionery." And where the man in "The Applicant" is described in terms of his black suit, here the men are described in terms of their shoes, present in the anonymity of hotel corridors, where

> Hands will be opening doors and setting
>
> Down shoes for a polish of carbon
> Into which broad toes will go tomorrow.

People accrete to their things, are absorbed into their artifacts. Finally, they lose all sense of a whole self and become atomized. Parts of them connect to their shoes, parts to their suit, part to their lace curtains, part to their icebox, and so on. There is nothing left; they have become reified and dispersed into a cluttered artificial landscape of their own production.

Because it is a kind of world created by men rather than women, because men are in control of the forces of production, Plath sees men as having first culpability for this state of affairs which affects both men and women. But men have gone further than this in their desire to change and control the world around them. In "The Munich Mannequins," man has finally transformed woman into a puppet, a mannequin, something that reflects both his disgust with and his fear of women. A mannequin cannot have children, but neither does it have that messy, terrifying, and incomprehensible blood flow each month. Mannequins are always beautiful, they don't talk, they can be carried around and manipulated into whatever form the situation requires; finally, they are created by man.

Mannequins (women, little men, in Lévi-Strauss's terms "a child's doll," which "can be grasped, assessed and apprehended at a glance") do away with the problem of female creativity and self-determination entirely.[23] Indeed, they are perfect. Trapped inside this vision, the speaker of the late poems often sees herself caught between nature and society, biology and intellect, her self-definition and the expectations of others, as between two mirrors.

Discussion of Sylvia Plath's late poems has often centered around her more shocking images. Yet the images of wars and concentration camps, of mass and individual violence, are only the end result of an underlying depersonalization, an abdication of people to their artifacts, and an economic and social structure that equates people and objects. Like the paper doll woman in "The Applicant," Sylvia Plath was doubly alienated from such a world, doubly objectified by it, and as a woman artist, doubly isolated within it.

What happens to human relationships in such a world? Is there any possibility of friendship, love, and beauty? The late poems which concern marriage all finally conclude that love is not possible; *The Bell Jar* and her poems about women show an equal estrangement.[24] For Plath, the one potentially uncorrupted and wholly positive love seems to be that between herself and her children, for at least in that relationship one person's perception is as yet unspoiled by a knowledge of the world it must live in. The opening line of "Child," a poem written the same day as "The Munich Mannequins," less than two weeks before she died, eschews all equivocation: "Your clear eye," she writes, "is the one absolutely beautiful thing." She wants to fill the child's sight with grand and classical images, she says, "not this troublous / Wringing of hands, this dark / Ceiling without a star." This is an embattled love and beauty, hemmed in and threatened on all sides.

A number of Plath's poems center upon her relationship with her children: In addition to "Child," "By Candlelight" (October 24, 1962), "For a Fatherless Son" (September 26, 1962), and "You're" (1960), "Balloons" (February 5, 1963), and "Nick and the Candlestick" (October 29, 1962). These poems should be distinguished from those like "Morning Song" and "Heavy Women," both written in 1961, which are about pregnancy and maternity and which focus on the self's reaction to the fact of childbirth rather than on the relationship between mother and child. *Three Women* is in this second group, concerned with the social defini-tions of pregnancy and childbirth and their effect upon women. Only with the Wife in that play do we see a continuing relation-ship between mother and child, and there the validity of the ex-perience is undercut as the Wife attempts to delude herself into believing that the outside world does not exist at all. In all the poems Plath wrote about her children and herself, mother and child exist in a closed-off world, a bubble outside the main stream of society. Whether metaphorized as a balloon or as a circle of lamplight, this peaceful world is limited both in space and dura-tion. The outside world, which is real, will eventually break through and destroy it; there is always a sense of threat and vulnerability. The contrast between these two worlds grows in the later poetry.

The precarious nature of this peace is explicit in "Nick and the Candlestick." Plath commented on this poem: "A mother nurses her baby son by candlelight and finds in him a beauty which, while it may not ward off the world's ill, does redeem her share of it."[25] The actual location of the poem is a room where her child is sleeping; the metaphorical location is a mine. Plath thor-oughly blends the two locations. The candle, like the canary, has been traditionally used by miners to test the amount of oxygen in the air. If the candle begins to sputter, as it does about halfway through the poem, that is a sign that the air is beginning to go. More obviously, the candle is a small circle of light in the midst of darkness. It is what we bring down into the mine from the world of sunlight above. As usual, Plath is ambivalent in the emo-tional deployment of her images. The cave is comforting because it is womb-like and limited in area and therefore comprehensible:

> Love, love,
> I have hung our cave with roses,
> With soft rugs—
>
> The last of Victoriana.

But the cave or mine is also terrifying with its "black bat airs," its white newts and fish like "panes of ice." The candlelight in a dark room makes a cave in reverse, a cave of light in a world of darkness. But this cave that is lighted and peaceful is not secure.

It is temporary and continually threatened. The speaker of the poem says to her child, "The pain / You wake to is not yours" and "You are the one / Solid the spaces lean on, envious."

Like the circle of candlelight in "Nick and the Candlestick," balloons can provide a temporary beauty. What Plath chooses to focus on in "Balloons," one of her last poems, is the moment in which one is destroyed. The first four stanzas of the poem are a description of the balloons, an explanation of what they represent to the poet and, on a less analytical level, what they represent to the children. They are alive, "Guileless and clear, / Oval soul-animals." They shriek when attacked and run away to hide on the ceiling. They are in a different category than the "dead furniture," more like people. They represent freedom, delight, beauty. They excite a sense of wonder. They are compared to peacocks; they fulfill a human need for sheer nonutilitarian beauty. They allow the mind to play upon wishes and fantasies. But when, in the last two stanzas, the little boy bites into the balloon, mistaking fantasy for reality, "a funny pink world he might eat," he is left with reality alone and only the fragments of wishes: "a world clear as water. / A red / Shred in his little fist."

A poem like "Poppies in October" (27 October 1962), while it is not about Plath's relation to her children, is connected in mood and theme to that group of poems. For what characterizes all of them is the description of a realm of innocence and beauty—either startling or tranquil—of something wholly positive. And this realm is threatened or destroyed or in some way undercut by the world which surrounds it, which is, by and large, not beautiful. In "Nick and the Candlestick," the other world exists throughout the poem just outside the circle of candlelight and is a continual threat to the peace within that circle. In "Balloons," a more joyous poem, the world still breaks in or rather is broken into at the end of the poem when the child bites the balloon. In some ways, the world inside the apartment has been a world inside a balloon. But this estrangement from the world is here seen as positive, not negative as in the glass egg of "A Life" or as in the controlling metaphor of *The Bell Jar*. "Poppies in October" puts the startling beauty of the late-blooming flowers immediately, in the first lines of the poem, into a context which connects it to the larger and more unpleasant world with which it coexists. The poppies bloom, astonishingly, in October, in a world capped by a gray polluted sky and populated by "eyes / Dulled to a halt under bowlers." The poppies are more colorful than a city sunrise or "the woman in the ambulance / Whose red heart blooms through her coat so astoundingly—." Caught between the blood red of the poppies and the dull gray of the world is the "eye" of the poet, gathering apocalyptic symbols and wondering what she is in such a world.

STASIS AND PROCESS:
THE VORTEX

Either way we choose, the angry witch
will punish us for saying which is which;
     in fatal equilibrium
we poise on perilous poles that freeze us in
a cross of contradiction, racked between
     the fact of doubt, the faith of dream.

Metamorphoses of the Moon (1953)

A number of Plath's late poems image the self caught up in a maelstrom of movement, painfully, finally fatally, trying to maintain a state of equilibrium or balance between opposing forces. The self is often seen as the still center, the eye of a hurricane; it moves but at the same time is still, for it moves only in relation to the movement of the forces it is caught between. Investigation of the kind, quality, direction, and potentiality of movement possible for the self is a central concern of Plath's, especially in the late poetry. The tension between stasis and process is imaged in a number of ways in the late poems. In "Edge," "Death & Co.," and "The Moon and the Yew Tree," for example, the self is static and, in the first two of those poems, dead. The hospital imagery of "Tulips" depicts the persona of the poem as the center of an activity directed toward renewal and health. In the bee poems the image is of the hive, immortal and cyclic, highly social, centered around the queen. In poems such as "Elm" and "Ariel," the self is poised at the middle of a vortex of movement.

How Plath defines this vortex is implicit in "Contusion," written in the last week of her life. The poem begins with a bruise:

"Color floods to the spot, dull purple. / The rest of the body is all washed out, / The color of pearl." "Contusion" is similar to two earlier poems, "The Eye Mote" and "Man in Black" (*The Colossus*) in its use of centering. It is like "Cut" in that it uses physical pain as the beginning of the poem's vision. In these four poems, and fairly consistently throughout Plath's poetry, what gives meaning to things is what obstructs them. What gives meaning to the normal is the abnormal. Perception occurs at a crisis point, where the speaker of the poem becomes aware of herself as a center of opposing tensions and where the meaning or purpose of existence is simply to maintain equilibrium. Each of the four stanzas of "Contusion" contains an apocalyptic image that seems at first to have little relation to the other three: the bruise, the hollowed rock around which "the sea sucks obsessively," a fly crawling down the wall, the ocean sliding its sheeted mirrors closed. "Dull purple," the bruise or contusion of the first stanza, has taken all color and life from the rest of the body. It is the center of movement seen in terms of color in the same way that the fly crawling down the wall in the third stanza fixes and centers our perception of a room. What finally holds the poem together is its sea imagery; the obsessive sucking of the sea caught in a hollowed rock, the retreat of the ocean and the heart into itself: "The sea slides back, / The mirrors are sheeted." What the speaker of Plath's poems sees in these moments of perception, looking into water, looking into mirrors, is not so much chaos as a reversed and chilling logic.

In "Johnny Panic and the Bible of Dreams," a story written in 1961 and based on her experience as a part-time clerical worker typing up case histories of patients at Massachusetts General Hospital in Boston in 1958–59, Plath sees the dreams people have, the specific forms of their potential madness, as a more accurate index to them than is their social behavior. The dreams her clerical heroine tells us about in that story are often closely linked to the kind of work the dreamers do. A man who works for a ball bearing factory, for example,

dreams every night how he's lying on his back with a grain of sand on his chest. Bit by bit, this grain of sand grows bigger and bigger until it's as big as a fair-sized house and he can't draw breath. . . . A lot of people these days dream they're being run over or eaten by machines. They're the cagey ones who won't go on the subway or the elevators.[26]

She has her own dream, she says, an archetypal dream, the boiled down essence of all the dreams she's been recording.

In this dream there's a great half-transparent lake stretching away in every direction, too big for me to see the shores of it, if there are any shores, and I'm hanging over it, looking down from the glass belly of some helicopter. At the bottom of the lake—so deep I can only guess at the dark masses moving and heaving—are the real dragons. The ones that were around before men started living in caves and cooking meat over fires and figuring out the wheel and the alphabet. Enormous isn't the word for them; they've got more wrinkles than Johnny Panic himself. Dream about these long enough and your feet and hands shrivel away when you look at them too closely. The sun shrinks to the size of an orange, only chillier, and you've been living in Roxbury since the last ice age. No place for you but a room padded soft as the first room you knew of, where you can dream and float, float and dream, till at last you actually are back among those great originals and there's no point in any dreams at all.

It's into this lake people's minds run at night, brooks and gutter-trickles to one borderless common reservoir. It bears no resemblance to those pure sparkling blue sources of drinking water the suburbs guard more jealously than the Hope diamond in the middle of pinewoods and barbed fences. . . .

. . . Call the water what you will, Lake Nightmare, Bog of Madness, it's here the sleeping people lie and toss together among the props of their worst dreams, one great brotherhood, though each of them, waking, thinks himself singular, utterly apart.[27]

We are all potential converts of Johnny Panic, Plath implies, for we all participate in this brotherhood of nightmares, whether we admit it or not. As interesting as the archetypal elements of this dream of dreams are the social images Plath uses to describe it. Roxbury is one of Boston's black neighborhoods. The white suburbs of Boston, including Wellesley where Plath lived for ten years, do each have a "pond" set amidst trees, prohibited to swimmers, and the pride of its community. The narrator of "Johnny Panic and the Bible of Dreams" sees "those pure sparkling-blue sources

of drinking water" as maintained in large measure by self-delusion. She carefully distinguishes herself and her dream from those
suburban reservoirs and identifies instead with the sense of powerlessness—cold, no hands or feet—in the earlier image.

This powerlessness—as fact, as choice, sometimes as rest—is one
aspect of those late poems which try out a static relationship between self and world. These poems are the ones most obviously
about death, about the attainment of perfection through a stopping of process and the continual rebirth leading nowhere that is
the subject of many of the *Ariel* poems. "Death & Co." (November 14, 1962) and "Edge" (February 5, 1963) both focus on the
achievement of death by the speaker of the poem. There are three
characters in "Death & Co."; the woman who is the speaker of
the poem and the two aspects or avatars of death who are described as business partners. "Two, of course there are two. / It
seems perfectly natural now—." The first face of death is vindic-
tive and predatory. He is described as a condor and he wants to
consume her. His method is to chip away at her self-esteem, her
defensive armor. When it is gone, he can eat her.

> His beak
>
> Claps sideways: I am not his yet.
> He tells me how badly I photograph.
> He tells me how sweet
> The babies look in their hospital
> Icebox

The other face of death is self-enclosed and selfish. He does not
really care about her—"Bastard / Masturbating a glitter,"— except that "he wants to be loved." Plath, in an unpublished type-
script meant to introduce some of her poems for a radio broadcast, said of "Death & Co.":

This poem . . . is about the double or schizophrenic nature of death—
the marmoreal coldness of Blake's death mask, say, hand in glove with
the fearful softness of worms, water and the other katabolists. I image
these two aspects of death as two men, two business friends, who have
come to call.[28]

The business partners have come to offer a business deal, to offer death to the speaker of the poem like a set of encyclopedias or a real estate lot in Florida or some shares in a new company. One tries the hard sell while the other takes a soft line, seemingly indifferent. They work well together. Yet somehow the speaker of the poem has made her own death and lies there quietly while all this activity is going on above and around her. "I do not stir," she says.

> The frost makes a flower,
> The dew makes a star,
> The dead bell,
> The dead bell.
>
> Somebody's done for.

The struggle in "Death & Co." to, at least, choose one's own death is past by the time Plath writes "Edge" in the last week of her life. Because it renders death both as luxuriant repose and as art, "Edge" is perhaps the most frightening poem in *Ariel*. The language is so beautiful that the reader is seduced toward accepting the poem's conclusion. The mood is calm, even peaceful. The speaker of the poem describes in a detached and slow, almost incantatory rhythm, a woman who is already dead. The poem has the quality of a still photograph.

> The woman is perfected.
> Her dead
>
> Body wears the smile of accomplishment,
> The illusion of a Greek necessity
>
> Flows in the scrolls of her toga,
> Her bare
>
> Feet seem to be saying:
> We have come so far, it is over.

"The woman is perfected." One of the three one-line sentences in the poem, it carries the poem's theme: Death is equivalent to stasis, and stasis, a stopping of process with its continual imperfections and need for rebirth, is perfection of a sort. Like "Death & Co.,"

"Edge" has three "characters"; though here, where the people are already dead, it is easier to see them as part of the setting. First is the dead woman, then the two children, also dead, whom she has folded "back into her body as petals / Of a rose close when the garden / Stiffens." Finally, the moon acts in this poem both as participant/character and as metaphor. As an earlier version of the opening line makes clear, "Edge" is from the moon's perspective: "Down there the woman is perfected."[29] In addition to the moon, there are two major metaphors in the poem: The dead woman and children are described as a Greek statue and they are also described in terms of a garden at night. In both cases, we receive an impression of a bare, cold landscape, the marble statue, the harsh moonlight, the stiff flowers which do not give off their odors but bleed them.

The poem's central image—the stone-like woman with her children gathered back into her body—Plath had thought of years before. In a 1955 letter, she wrote:

At midnight, when the moon makes blue lizard scales of roof shingles. . . . the hungry cosmic mother sees the world shrunk to embryo again and her children gathered sleeping back into the dark, huddling in bulbs and pods, pale and distant as the folded bean seed to her full milky love which freezes across the sky in a crucifix of stars.[30]

In this initial statement of the image, the "hungry cosmic mother," a vampiric figure familiar in Plath's late poetry, is a primal goddess, a world creator who becomes a world destroyer, reabsorbing her children and the world, turning back time to embryo and chaos. Eight years later, in "Edge," Plath divides this goddess into two characters: on the one hand, the dead woman with her children, who somehow remains human and sympathetic for us even as she takes on the quality of stone, and on the other hand, the detached, hooded, and cynical moon, staring down at the scene, neither helping nor hindering.

The moon in "Edge" is a later avatar of what Plath in *The Colossus* had called her "disquieting muses." The attitude of the moon toward this particular scene is not necessarily approval, closer to indifference.

The moon has nothing to be sad about,
Staring from her hood of bone.

She is used to this sort of thing.
Her blacks crackle and drag.

"Edge" begins with the dead woman but it ends with the moon, which represents the kind of death, stasis, and perfection the woman in the poem has wanted to achieve. The moon, by earthly standards, is dead, airless, lifeless, and static. Nothing can happen there. Yet it is the moon which causes movement on the earth—the tides and, symbolically, monthly menstruation. Static itself, the moon is in control of movement going on outside it, down there on earth. "Staring from her hood of bone," the moon is a powerful presence in this poem. The woman in the poem, having chosen her own death, has taken on stone/bone/moon qualities and with those some of the moon's power.

An earlier poem, "The Moon and the Yew Tree" (October 22, 1961) helps to give the reader a social context for Plath's final choice of death and stasis. Like "The Couriers" (November 4, 1962), "The Moon and the Yew Tree" distinguishes between false and true signs. In "The Couriers," a false sign was marriage: "A ring of gold with the sun in it? / Lies. Lies and a grief." A true sign was "a disturbance in mirrors, / The sea shattering its gray one—." Here the true couriers are the moon and the yew tree and the false courier is the church, with its promise of resurrection and tenderness.

The actual geographical location of the poem is the country house in Devon that Sylvia Plath and Ted Hughes bought in the summer of 1961 and where she lived until a few days before Christmas 1962. The house faced a twelfth-century Anglican church. In a story called "The Mother's Union," Plath describes the relation of the house to the church:

The front door, yellow-painted and flanked by two pungent bushes of box, faced across an acre of stinging nettles to where the church indicated a gray heaven above its scallop of surrounding headstones. The front gate opened just under the corner of the graveyard.
    . . . The gravestones, greenly luminous in the thick dusk, looked as if their ancient lichens might possess some magical power of phospho-

rescence. The two women passed under the churchyard, with its flat, black yew.[31]

The speaker of the poem must choose between the moon, "bald and wild," and the church, with its human, tamed, and organized approach to the unknown. The church bells affirm a resurrection, she says in the second stanza, but the moon, a true courier, does not promise anything beyond itself. "The moon is no door. It is a face in its own right"; "it is quiet / With the O-gape of complete despair. I live here." The church also promises tenderness, mercy, and mildness. But the speaker of the poem does not believe this. Like the disquieting muses of an earlier poem, who stood in opposition to the speaker's mother and self-delusion, here the poet again chooses what she sees as real, if terrifying, rather than what is pleasant and comforting, but false. "The moon is my mother," she says. "She is not sweet like Mary." In the last stanza of "The Moon and the Yew Tree," she contrasts the effigies of the saints inside the church, cold blue and "stiff with holiness," to her two real muses: "The moon sees nothing of this. She is bald and wild. / And the message of the yew tree is blackness—blackness and silence."

The moon, the yew tree, the old church with its graveyard, and the speaker of the poem all become deliberately confused and blended into each other. The poem opens: "This is the light of the mind, cold and planetary. / The trees of the mind are black. The light is blue." In one sense, the landscape of the poem is the mind, containing the cold and planetary moon, the black yew trees, and the blue light of the church. Marjorie Perloff and Jon Rosenblatt have each remarked that the "I" of Sylvia Plath's poems projects her own internal landscape out on to the world and subsumes it.[32] The "I" of Sylvia Plath's poems often feels herself being lodged in or accreted upon things in the world. However, in many of Sylvia Plath's poems the opposite process occurs. The self often feels itself in danger of being swallowed up by the object perceived. In *The Divided Self*, R. D. Laing discusses the fear of implosion as "the *impingement* of reality. Impingement does not convey, however, the full terror of the experience of the world as liable at any moment to crash in and obliterate all identity as a gas will rush in and obliterate a vacuum."[33] The relative isolation or

engagement of the self with the world around it is more complicated than at first appears. And often, the poems' conclusions are
like that of the speaker of "The Moon and the Yew Tree," who
says: "I simply cannot see where there is to get to." Where she is
now is a static place; the four—the moon, the church, the yew
tree, the speaker of the poem—are fixed in some immovable schema
relative to each other and perhaps even to the rest of the world.

This inability to move is also characteristic of "Elm" (April 19,
1962; originally titled "The Elm Speaks"), where the perspective
is from inside the tree. Here the elm, which cannot itself move, is
the center of a whirlwind of activity pressing on the speaker of
the poem from within and without. Plath had written earlier, in
1956, on the difficulty of conjuring up a dryad; but here the elm
speaks in its own person to the poet in the first four stanzas of the
poem, establishing a congruence between the poet's situation and
its own. "I know the bottom," she says. "I know it with my
great tap root: / It is what you fear." She asks the poet whether it
is the sea she thinks she hears or the voice of her own madness.
By the fifth stanza, a third of the way through the poem, the
"you" form of address has been all but dropped. The poet has
fused with the elm and in the next stanzas undergoes a trial by
sun, wind, and moon from the outside and by equal turbulance
from within. "I have suffered the atrocity of sunsets," she says,
and "Now I break up in pieces that fly about like clubs."

> I am inhabited by a cry.
> Nightly it flaps out
> Looking, with its hooks, for something to love.
>
> I am terrified by this dark thing
> That sleeps in me;
> All day I feel its soft, feathery turnings, its malignity.

By this time the elm tree has taken on the characteristics of the
poet, but it is equally important that the poet has taken on the
characteristics of the tree. The medusa-like face which looks out
from the branches at the end is another apocalyptic vision; it could
be either a nightmare perceived by the poet or the poet herself and
is probably both. Whichever it is, the effect is to turn the viewer
into stone ("it petrifies the will"). And stone, an image central to

The Colossus poems, is even more immovable and static, even further removed from the human, than is the elm tree.

The emphasis in "Elm" is on the static nature of the vortex. The poet becomes the tree, and the end of the poem hints at a further metamorphosis into an even more static substance—stone. In contrast, the title poem of *Ariel* focuses on the dynamic nature of the vortex. "Ariel" (October 27, 1962) begins with the words "stasis in darkness," and the poem progresses from stasis to movement and from darkness to light. Literally an account of a gallop on a horse named Ariel, it is one of the more compact and abstract, obscure and Emily Dickinson–like poems in this volume. It does not have the conversational rhythms of ordinary or heightened speech which characterize "Tulips," "Lady Lazarus," "Daddy," or "Elm"; it is not the "direct, and even plain, speech" characteristic of most of the poems in *Ariel*.[34] The language is fragmented and compact; a phrase stands for a sentence and a word for a phrase. In other ways too it is abstract or metaphysical, like the apocalyptic "Apprehensions" (May 28, 1962). "Ariel" attempts to describe an experience in which concreteness and materiality are both shed and transcended through a merging with immediate experience. The post merges with the horse through the medium of their shared speed: "God's lioness, / How one we grow, / Pivot of heels and knees!—." At the same time, she shucks off all that is irrelevant to the present: "The child's cry / Melts in the wall." She uses the same image as in "Lady Lazarus" when she says, "White / Godiva, I unpeel— / Dead hands, dead stringencies." Even more than in "Lady Lazarus," which ends with the persona's red-haired and angry phoenix-like rebirth, here in "Ariel" the poet escapes the cycle of death and rebirth and becomes transformed into something bodiless though not dispersed.

And I
Am the arrow,

The dew that flies
Suicidal, at one with the drive
Into the red

Eye, the cauldron of morning.

The horse and the train are the two major images of linear movement in the late poems. The train, an essential component of Plath's war poems, signifies man-made movement. It has a certain grandeur because of the size and power of the engine and because the track is there even when the train is not, an intention engraved upon the land. In the *Ariel* poems, the sound of the train is terrifying. Often, the people in the train are being transported to their death, either as soldiers going to the front lines or as prisoners being taken to concentration camps. In "Daddy," the train is "An engine, an engine / Chuffing me off like a Jew / A Jew to Dachau, Auschwitz, Belsen." And the sound of the train is incorporated into the rhythm of the poem. The train is usually a negative image of movement, and in "Totem" (January 28, 1963) Plath juxtaposes the inexorability of its movement with the questionable significance of its destination. "The engine is killing the track, the track is silver, / It stretches into the distance. It will be eaten nevertheless. / Its running is useless." All of "Getting There" (November 6, 1962) is a train ride through a surrealistic landscape of dead bodies and parts of bodies, the train a monstrous animal and herself moving through this terror to a rebirth in forgetfulness. "Is there no still place," she asks. "Turning and turning in the middle air, / Untouched and untouchable." The train is an artifact, and the landscape the train moves through is cluttered with the results of various human instruments of destruction. In contrast, the horse in "Ariel," which also stands for speed and for power, is seen more positively, its movement more exhilarating, the speaker more part of it, less passive. At the end of "Getting There" the speaker of the poem is reborn "pure as a baby," but she has had to undergo a tremendous amount of perceptual suffering first. She does get there, but the getting there is almost more than she can bear, and the goal is nothing particularly admirable, simply a Lethe-like blankness. In contrast, in "Ariel" the process of movement is what is important and the end of movement is purposely left vague, though its quality is heroic, transcendent, and apocalyptic.

The choice between process and stasis which Sylvia Plath set herself in her late poems is complex, multidimensional, and not easily resolved. If stasis implies rest, escape, and a kind of perfection, it also means an acceptance of powerlessness and an admission that there is no place to go. Process, on the other hand, combines the exhilaration of movement with the sense that one is going somewhere, since movement suggests purpose; but it also implies the dangerous possibilities of chaos and speed, and the danger—to a woman as intellectual as Plath—of giving oneself up to motion while still unsure of the goal. That even the exhilarating movement of "Ariel" is finally seen as "suicidal" suggests the ambivalence in Plath's attitude. This uncertainty about the end result of movement, given the kind of fragmented and brutalized world symbolized by the image of the train in her late poems, is what finally makes the choice between stasis and movement unbearable.

PURITY AND REBIRTH

In the depersonalized, bureaucratized society that Sylvia Plath images sometimes as an office or hospital and sometimes as a concentration camp, there is no possibility of a complete, whole, integrated, and healthy love between two people. In an authoritarian social structure that denies self-definition and growth to women, love between man and woman fails; and this failure stands, in Plath's poems, for the failure of human relationships in general. The kind of love Plath images in the poems from 1961 on is both the consequence of and the metaphor for a decayed society.

Though Caliban is never explicitly mentioned in Sylvia Plath's late poetry, while Ariel, that light, androgynous incarnation of grace and movement is, Caliban's implicit presence is strong. In *The Tempest* (which Plath had earlier alluded to in "Full Fathom Five"), Caliban and Ariel can both be seen as possibilities for humankind: the animal and the soul, the bestial and the transcendent, ugliness and beauty. Both are in thrall to the magician Prospero, but while Ariel moves throughout the play toward earning his/her freedom, Caliban slides from one form of slavery to another.

Though set on a remote and magical island, the world of *The Tempest* is governed by assumptions both patriarchal and mercantile. Miranda, Prospero's daughter, is a valuable object which Prospero "sells" in order to buy back his title and his place in the world outside the island. Ariel, in obligation to Prospero for freeing her from Sycorax's spell, is forced to bargain for her own freedom from Prospero. Caliban has nothing to sell except his hate for Prospero, and since Prospero is in control of the "currency" of his island, Caliban's attempts to make a "sale" to the shipwrecked nobles fail abysmally. While Ariel moves toward freedom, Caliban is trapped by his male biology in the same way Miranda is trapped by her female biology. However, unlike Miranda, Caliban is neither female nor beautiful. One comes away from *The Tempest* with a certain sympathy for Caliban who, in a proto-capitalist economy, has no capital.

What Plath seems to have borrowed from *The Tempest* is the insight that Caliban is not so much a discrete monster as an important aspect of the ruler of the island, Prospero. Caliban is that aspect of an Apollonian, patriarchal culture which represents a perversion of reason or perhaps a grounding of what we define as reason in male sexuality or biology. Ariel, on the other hand, is an androgynous presence, a being who seems to have transcended biology and the traps of sexual definition. Prospero has control over Ariel only for a limited time; he is much more entangled with Caliban. There are glimpses in Plath's late poems, for example in "Daddy" and "Death & Co.," of the earthbound, static, heavy, bestial, and unbeautiful figure of Caliban. In "Death & Co." we see both sides—Prospero and Caliban—of the male other which represents for Plath the patriarchal, authoritarian, reason-bound culture within which she must try to discover her own possibilities for self, a culture where she feels trapped inside social definitions of her own female biology.

Purity in the *Ariel* poems operates on two levels: the biological/psychological and the social/mystical. Caliban's implicit presence operates most obviously in Plath's late work as a sexual threat: the possibility of rape. The psychological dimension of this sexual threat is, finally and most essentially, a concern for the integrity of one's inner space. This is a major theme of *The Bell Jar*, where to lose one's virginity is, quite literally, to be in danger of bleeding to death. Thus the emphasis on purity, both in the novel and the late poems, suggests at the same time a need to be defined non-biologically and a longing for wholeness, solitude, integrity and control of self.

The personae of Sylvia Plath's poems, the heroines of her monomyth, are searching for a particular kind of rebirth: a transformed self reborn into a transformed world. The difficulty is that they are trying to accomplish this transformation from within a set of assumptions that severely limits the possibility. As a result, integrity of self is often defined in Plath's late poetry as "purity." And purity is defined, often, as sensory deprivation, as either detachment or numbness, a wish to be "nunhearted and blind to the world" ("Barren Woman") or as death, the dead body of a woman wearing a "smile of accomplishment" ("Edge"). Longings for numbness or death are passive responses to entrapment. More active attempts to break out of this set of patriarchal assumptions, to find another alternative, often take the form of a self-image as a Mother Goddess figure of personal and social vengeance, like those who appear at the end of "Lady Lazarus" and "Stings." Robert Graves writes that in our "Apollonian civilization" the Goddess cannot return "until women themselves grow weary of a decadent patriarchalism."[35] Caliban and Prospero are the two sides of this decadent patriarchalism; the crucial dimension that Plath adds to the figure of Caliban is that his deformity and his brutality are the result of an intellectual and social perversion. The perversion of sexuality through violence and the concomitant impossibility of love are both a metaphor for and an aspect of a larger social brutality and decay which affects her own possibilities for rebirth. The impossibility of a healthy love relationship and its roots in a violently one-sided and therefore perverse social structure is the subject of three poems Plath recorded together in 1962: "Fever 103°" (October 20, 1962), "Lady Lazarus" (October 23–29, 1962), and "Daddy" (October 12, 1962).

This is the theme of a number of contemporary American women poets. Since 1966, Denise Levertov has often made the same kind of connection Plath did about the possibilities of love between people, particularly between men and women, within a larger social context based on principles inimical to such love. Levertov's 1966 poem, "Life at War," suggests the vitiating effect the Vietnam War had upon our own consciousness. "The same war / continues," Levertov writes.

> We have breathed the grits of it in, all our lives,
> our lungs are pocked with it,
> the mucous membrane of our dreams

> coated with it, the imagination
> filmed over with the gray filth of it.

And she ends that poem by making the connection between the personal and the social explicit.

> Yes, this is the knowledge that jostles for space
> in our bodies along with all we
> go on knowing of joy, of love;
>
> our nerve filaments twitch with its presence
> day and night,
> nothing we say has not the husky phlegm of it in the saying,
> nothing we do has the quickness, the sureness,
> the deep intelligence living at peace would have.[36]

Ihab Hassan says, correctly, of the *Ariel* poems that "they move beyond their own center of fear toward some reconciliation in love that Sylvia Plath is never permitted to reach."[37] The possibilities for a reconciliation in love are severely limited in a world which contains, for Levertov, the tiger cages and napalm of the Vietnam War, and for Plath, the atomic bomb and the concentration camps of World War II. Any relationship that does exist in such a world does so by dulling awareness, by pretending that this other does not exist. And for Plath and Levertov both, to dull awareness is to already be one of the undead.

It is this kind of negative awareness, that is, a painful consciousness of a cultural decay and violence that vitiates the possibility of love, that structures "Fever 103°." The poem begins by asking for a definition of purity and immediately plunges into a description of what purity is not. In the kind of world we now inhabit, the mythological and Christian hells have lost their meaning and their force; real life is worse than anyone could have imagined hell to be. "The tongues of hell / Are dull," Plath writes,

> dull as the triple
>
> Tongues of dull, fat Cerberus
> Who wheezes at the gate. Incapable
> Of licking clean
>
> The aguey tendon, the sin, the sin.

There is no possibility of redemption, at least not through the old routes. In a less complicated time, John Donne could define both love and God by what they were not. The argumentative structure Donne used in his poem "Negative Love" dates back to the Upanishads: "Neti, neti"—God is not this, not that. The assumption behind negative theology is that God is so all encompassing, so omnipresent, that the only way you can begin to describe Him is through isolating what He is not. Donne exalts his secular love by giving it a similar divine status. In "Fever 103°" Plath tries to define purity by pointing out what it is not, but finds by the end of the poem that she has defined it away. In her search for a rebirth into purity and an escape from the cycle of suicide and rebirth into the same unchanged world, Plath considers in "Fever 103°" history, nature, art, and religion and finds in none of them any trace of what she is seeking. In the reference to the ineffectuality of Cerberus, she considers pre-Christian theology and, in a stanza on the recording but left out of the version of the poem published in *Ariel*, she refers to medieval Christianity in terms of the Inquisition: "O auto-da-fé / The purple men, gold-crusted, thick with spleen / Sit with their hooks and crooks and stoke the light." The possibility of a redemption through Christian love seems, then, to be what is first undercut in the poem. Her method is to place the theological principles and theory within a practical and historical context.

The next six stanzas turn to images of a more contemporary world. Isadora Duncan's scarf caught in the wheel of a car and strangling her turns into "yellow sullen smokes," the residue of the victims of twentieth century imperialism, which:

> make their own element. They will not rise,
>
> But trundle round the globe
> Choking the aged and meek,
> The weak
>
> Hothouse baby in its crib

The Christian references in this section suggest a continuing history of the perversion of religious principles and the reasons that religion cannot be an escape route. The "ghastly orchid" of the next line turns into a mushroom cloud of radiation, which in turn becomes ash: "Greasing the bodies of adulterers / Like Hiroshima ash and eating in. / The sin. The sin." The modulation from one image to another in the first part of "Fever 103°" is beautifully controlled and produces an accumulated effect of nausea leading up to herself and her present situation. That is, all of these public events are factors in her own life; the individual does not exist outside the context of the events of her or his age.

The mental sickness that is apparent in public and historical events cannot help but carry over into one's private life, spoiling it. The speaker of the poem is sick, both in body and mind; her sickness is a reflection of a social condition. "Darling, all night / I have been flickering, off, on, off, on. / The sheets grow heavy as a lecher's kiss." Addressed to a lover, the poem is an explanation of the impossibility of love or, in a larger sense, of any kind of affirmation or celebration. The poet's response to this situation is to try to disengage; to become pure seems to mean this. But the method of disengagement imaged here is not offered as a serious solution. "I think I am going up," she says.

> I think I may rise—
> The beads of hot metal fly, and I, love, I
>
> Am a pure acetylene
> Virgin
> Attended by roses,
>
> By kisses, by cherubim,
> By whatever these pink things mean.

The poem mocks the image of a traditional Christian transcendence. Offered in terms of twentieth-century commercialism, Christianity here becomes a Hallmark greeting card. Moreover, the rising to purification through fire has already been undercut in the poem by the auto-da-fé, by "the indelible smell / Of a snuffed candle," and by the "yellow sullen smokes"; fire means, both here and in other poems by Plath, not purification but the gas ovens of Auschwitz. And one does not escape in any case, but is doomed to remain as a yellow pall circling the earth. Since the metaphysical can, finally, only be defined in reference to a particular indi-

vidual acting within a particular social context, this ostensible
Christian transformation is not offered as a real solution. The conclusion of "Fever 103°" is bitterly ironic.

Two other transformations are suggested more seriously, if in
less detail, in "Fever 103°": into artifice and into nature. "I am a
lantern—," she writes. "My head a moon / Of Japanese paper,
my gold beaten skin / Infinitely delicate and infinitely expensive."
The possibility of an escape into the static perfection of artifice
again connects Plath to Yeats, particularly "Sailing to Byzantium," where he writes:

> and gather me
> Into the artifice of eternity.
>
> Once out of nature I shall never take
> My bodily form from any natural thing,
> But such a form as Grecian goldsmiths make
> Of hammered gold and gold enamelling
> To keep a drowsy Emperor awake;
> Or sit upon a golden bough to sing
> To lords and ladies of Byzantium
> Of what is past, or passing, or to come.[38]

However, even when attracted to and toying with the notion of
escaping into the timeless perfection of art, Yeats cannot entirely
forget the world. As a golden bird, he sings of temporality, "of
what is past, or passing, or to come." Neither can Sylvia Plath
forget the world, but this spoils rather than tempers her vision of
escape into purity. The self-image as lantern or artifice modulates
into a self-image as flower or nature. "Does not my heat astound
you. And my light. / All by myself I am a huge camellia / Glowing and coming and going, flush on flush." Neither the transformation into artifice nor the transformation into nature works here
because both self-images of heat and light and beauty are spoiled
by their connection to earlier images of social horror. Her self-
image as lantern is preceded by the "indelible smell / Of a snuffed
candle" and by the "yellow sullen smokes." The attempt to transform herself into something in nature is also undercut. The "huge
camellia / Glowing and coming and going, flush on flush" is only
another vision of the atomic bomb exploding; it is "the ghastly

orchid / Hanging its hanging garden in the air." Finally, the speaker of the poem cannot become anything that is not already spoiled by the larger social context. There is no possibility of escaping, of becoming something pure, because she is too implicated in her own historical context.

While "Fever 103°" is an analysis of the methodology of escape, a study of the traditional escape routes, and an explanation of why they no longer work, "Lady Lazarus" examines the condition of the self, trapped into a cycle of death and rebirth back into the same unchanged world.

> Dying
> Is an art, like everything else.
> I do it exceptionally well.
>
> I do it so it feels like hell.
> I do it so it feels real.
> I guess you could say I've a call.
>
> It's easy enough to do it in a cell.
> It's easy enough to do it and stay put.
> It's the theatrical
>
> Comeback in broad day
> To the same place, the same face, the same brute
> Amused shout:
>
> "A miracle!"
> That knocks me out.

"Lady Lazarus" defines a particularly brutal and dehumanizing relationship between the individual and her society. In spite of this, the poem has the vocal quality of a manifesto, a statement of purpose and intent, a self-assertion. Lady Lazarus, self-condemned to repeat endlessly the same cycle of suicide and rebirth, nevertheless still feels a certain pride in her tenacity. The persona of "Lady Lazarus" is defiant and, as in "The Applicant," the poem is addressed in part to the reader:

> The peanut-crunching crowd
> Shoves in to see
>
> Them unwrap me hand and foot—

The big strip tease.
Gentlemen, ladies

These are my hands
My knees.

"Lady Lazarus" describes the relationship between poet/performer and audience in a society which has separated creativity and consumption; we have, throughout the poem, an uneasy feeling that as readers we have been incorporated into the poem—we are all part of the peanut-crunching crowd.

To the crowd, the spectators, the speaker of this poem is an object. Though her pain is apparent, they make no attempt to help her; indeed, their watching is a sick thing, feeding off her emotion. They are seen in the guise of sensation seekers, perhaps needing the vicarious thrill of the poet's own emotions in order to feel that they themselves are alive. An earlier poem, collected in *The Colossus*, sets up a similar relationship between someone involved in a personal disaster and the others, who watch. The central figure of "Aftermath" is Medea, and Plath writes that, "cheated of the pyre and the rack, / The crown sucks her last tear and turns away." In "Lady Lazarus" the tone is, if possible, more bitter. Here there is no mediating Medea, but an "I" confronting its audience directly.

The crowd has no sense of her as a complete human being. She recognizes that they see her as fragments and surfaces:

These are my hands,
My knees.
I may be skin and bone,

Nevertheless, I am the same, identical woman.

The relationship between the crowd and the speaker of the poem in "Lady Lazarus" is similar to that between Bigger Thomas and the populace of Chicago hunting him in Richard Wright's *Native Son*. Bigger identifies himself with the murder he has committed, although it was not something he meant to do. He says, "What I killed for, I am."[39] Bigger's murder of Mary Dalton and the suicides of Lady Lazarus both become an assertion of wholeness, an act of self-definition, and a last desperate act of contempt toward the peanut-crunching crowd. This contempt, which is also a kind of self-contempt, reaches its height in the poem in her offer to sell tickets to the crowd: "There is a charge / For the eyeing of my scars." Throughout, the speaker of "Lady Lazarus" equates herself with the Jewish victims of Nazi Germany and the crowd, that is, us, with those who watched, horrified but implicated in the act because for a long time we did nothing to stop it, since, we thought, it had nothing to do with us. The deader, more dehumanized, more isolated people become, the more horror it takes to elicit any kind of response. A. Alvarez writes that what matters in the concentration camps

is not so much the physical torture . . . but the way modern, as it were industrial, techniques can be used to destroy utterly the human identity. Individual suffering can be heroic provided it leaves the person who suffers a sense of his own individuality—provided, that is, there is an illusion of choice remaining to him. But when suffering is mass-produced, men and women become as equal and identityless as objects on an assembly line.[40]

The center of "Lady Lazarus" is the dehumanized relationship between self-image and image of the world, between the speaker of the poem and her audience.

"Lady Lazarus" is addressed directly—over the heads of the peanut-crunching crowd—to five aspects of the same figure: Herr God, Herr Lucifer, Herr Doktor, Herr Enemy, and in a line left out of the version published in *Ariel* but on the recording, Herr Professor. Obviously, the structure within which Lady Lazarus is committing these repeated suicides and making these repeated comebacks to the same place is a patriarchal one. Heaven, hell, and the professions are seen as a male structure, to which in the last lines of the poem she delivers a warning:

> Herr God, Herr Lucifer
> Beware
> Beware.
>
> Out of the ash
> I rise with my red hair
> And I eat men like air.

Somehow, if she can ever break out of this cycle which brings her back to the same body and the same place over and over, her transformed being will be dedicated to vengeance. That this is also seen as a potential escape from the cycle is clear when the phoenix-like rebirth from the ashes in the last lines of "Lady Lazarus" is compared to the arrow that flies suicidal "into the red / Eye, the cauldron of morning" at the end of "Ariel" and to the triumphant flight of the queen, "with her lion-red body," in "Stings."

The kind of relationship between self and society, poet and audience, which Plath images in "Lady Lazarus," is metaphorized in explicitly sexual terms. The "I" of the poem, who acts, is surrounded by a circle of voyeurs. The violence of her suicide attempts is equated, in the response of the slack-jawed and dull-eyed audience, with a strip tease. "Daddy" also identifies sexuality with violence. "Every woman adores a Fascist, / The boot in the face, the brute / Brute heart of a brute like you."

While the metaphor for the depersonalization and alienation of the individual from society is, in "Lady Lazarus," a kind of impersonal voyeurism, the particular sexual metaphor in "Daddy" is sado-masochism, which stands for the authority structure of a patriarchal and war-making society. And while "Fever 103°" describes the failure of the traditional modes of rebirth, and "Lady Lazarus" examines the condition of the individual trapped in herself and her society, "Daddy" is an analysis of the structure of the society in which the individual is enmeshed. Intertwined with the image of sadist and masochist in "Daddy" is a parallel image of vampire and victim. In "Daddy," father, husband, and a larger patriarchal and competitive authority structure, which the speaker of the poem sees as having been responsible for the various imperialisms of the twentieth century, all melt together and become demonic, finally a gigantic vampire figure. In the modulation from one image to another to form an accumulated image that is characteristic of many of Plath's late poems, the male figure at the center of "Daddy" takes four major forms: the statue, the Gestapo officer, the professor, and the vampire. The poem begins, however, with an image of a black shoe, an image which, like the black shoe in "The Munich Mannequins" and like the black suit in "The Applicant," can be seen to stand for corporate man. The second stanza of the poem refers back to the title poem of *The*

Colossus, where the speaker's father, representative of a gigantic male other, so dominated her world that her horizon was bounded by his scattered pieces. In "Daddy," she describes him as:

> Marble-heavy, a bag full of God,
> Ghastly statue with one grey toe
> Big as a Frisco seal
>
> And a head in the freakish Atlantic
> Where it pours bean green over blue
> In the waters off beautiful Nauset.

Between "The Colossus" and "Daddy" there has been a move-ment from a mythic and natural landscape to one with social and political boundaries. Here the image of her father, grown larger than the earlier Colossus of Rhodes, stretches across and subsumes the whole of the United States, from the Pacific to the Atlantic ocean.

The next seven stanzas of "Daddy" construct the image of the Gestapo officer, using her family background—her parents were both of German origin—to mediate between her personal sense of suffocation and the social history of the Nazi invasions. The black shoe of the first stanza in which she says she has been wedged like a foot "barely daring to breathe" becomes in stanza ten, at the end of the Nazi section, a larger social image of suffocation: "Not God but a swastika / So black no sky could squeak through." The Gestapo figure recurs briefly three stanzas later as the speaker of the poem transfers the image from father to husband and inciden-tally suggests that the victim has some control in a brutalized as-sociation—at least to the extent she chooses to be there.[41]

> I made a model of you,
> A man in black with a Meinkampf look
>
> And a love of the rack and the screw.
> And I said I do, I do.

The Gestapo figure becomes "Herr Professor" in stanza eleven, an actual image of Plath's father, and also an image of what has for centuries been seen as the prototypical and even ideal relationship between a man and a woman.[42] The professor, who is a man, talks and is active; the woman, who is a student, listens and is passive. A patriarchal social structure is at its purest and, superficially, at its most benign in the stereotyped relationship of male teacher and female student and is a stock romantic fantasy even in women's literature—Emma and Mr. Knightley, Lucy Snowe and the professor in *Villette*.[43] But Plath places this image between the images of Nazi/Jew and vampire/victim so that it becomes the center of a series. Indeed, the image of daddy as teacher turns almost immediately into a devil/demon/vampire:

> A cleft in your chin instead of your foot
> But no less a devil for that, no not
> Any less the black man who
>
> Bit my pretty red heart in two.

The last two stanzas of "Daddy" are like the conclusion of "Lady Lazarus" in their assertion that the speaker of the poem is breaking out of the cycle and that, in order to do so, she must turn on and kill Herr God, Herr Lucifer in the one poem, and Daddy in his final metamorphosis as vampire in the other poem. Plath explained this in Freudian terms in an introductory note to the poem for a BBC Third Programme reading:

The poem is spoken by a girl with an Electra complex. The father died while she thought he was God. Her case is complicated by the fact that her father was also a Nazi and her mother very possibly part Jewish. In the daughter the two strains marry and paralyze each other—she has to act out the awful little allegory once over before she is free of it.[44]

This reenacting of the allegory becomes at the end of "Daddy" a frenzied communal ritual of exorcism.

> Daddy, you can lie back now.
>
> There's a stake in your fat black heart
> And the villagers never liked you.
> They are dancing and stamping on you.
> They always *knew* it was you.
> Daddy, daddy, you bastard, I'm through.

This cycle of victim/vampire is, left alone, a closed and repetitious cycle, like the repeated suicides of "Lady Lazarus." According to the legends and the Hollywood film versions of these legends we all grew up on, once consumed by a vampire, one dies and is reborn a vampire and preys upon others, who in their turn die and become vampires. The vampire imagery in Sylvia Plath's poetry intersects on one level with her World War II imagery and its exploitation and victimization and on another level intersects with her images of a bureaucratic, fragmented, and dead—in the sense of numbed and unaware—society. The connections are sometimes confused, but certainly World War II is often imaged in her poetry as a kind of grisly, vampiric feast. In "Fever 103°," for example, she writes of "Greasing the bodies of adulterers / Like Hiroshima ash and eating in. / The sin. The sin." And "Mary's Song" (November 19, 1962), which begins with an image of a lamb roast crackling in the oven, quickly moves to

> The same fire
>
> Melting the tallow heretics,
> Ousting the Jews.
> Their thick palls float
>
> Over the cicatrix of Poland, burnt-out
> Germany.
> They do not die.

The victims do not die, but stay as the "yellow sullen smokes" of "Fever 103°"—a form of spiritual pall, an accumulation of guilt that will in its turn affect subsequent generations.

The whole of "Daddy" is an exorcism to banish the demon, put a stake through the vampire's heart, and thus break the cycle of vampire→victim. It is crucial to the poem that the exorcism is accomplished through communal action by the "villagers." The rhythm of the poem is powerfully and deliberately primitive: a child's chant, a formal curse. The hard sounds, short lines, and repeated rhymes of "do," "you," "Jew," and "through" give a hard pounding quality to the poem that is close to the sound of a heart beat. "Daddy," as well as "Lady Lazarus" and, to a lesser extent, "Fever 103°," is structured as a magical formula or incantation. In *The Colossus* poems, Plath also used poetry as a ritual incantation, but in those early poems it was most often directed toward transformation of self. By 1961, she is less often attempting to transform self into some other, but rather attempting to rid herself and her world of demons. That is, rebirth cannot occur until after the demons have been exorcised. In all three of these poems, the possibilities of the individual are very much tied to those of her society.

Purity, which is what exorcism aims at, is for Plath an ambiguous concept. On the one hand it means integrity of self, wholeness rather than fragmentation, as unspoiled state of being, rest, perfection, aesthetic beauty, and loss of self through transformation into some reborn other. On the other hand, it also means absence, isolation, blindness, a kind of autism which shuts out the world, stasis and death, and a loss of self through dispersal into some other. In "Lady Lazarus" and "Fever 103°" the emphasis is on exorcising the poet's previous selves, though within a social context that makes that unlikely. "Daddy," however, is a purification of the world; in "Daddy" it is the various avatars of the other—the male figure who represents the patriarchal society she lives in—that are being exorcised. In all three cases, the exorcism is violent and, perhaps, provisional. Does she believe, in any of these cases, that a rebirth under such conditions is really possible, that an exorcism is truly taking place, that once the allegory is reenacted, she will be rid of it? The more the speaker of the poems defines her situation as desperate, the more violent and vengeful becomes the agent of purification and transformation. All three of these poems are retaliatory fantasies: in "Lady Lazarus" she swallows men, in "Fever 103°" she leaves them behind, in "Daddy" she kills them. Robert Graves wrote in *The White Goddess* that our culture must again learn to acknowledge the Goddess,

but the longer the change is delayed, and therefore the more exhausted by man's irreligious improvidence the natural resources of soil and sea become, the less placid and merciful will be the five-fold mask that the Goddess ultimately assumes.[45]

Throughout the *Ariel* poems, Sylvia Plath uses mythical, magical characters and narratives, some of them traditional figures, some of her own creation. There is a crucial distinction, however, between how she had used mythology in the early poems and how she uses it in the late poems. In the early poems it was both more and less conscious than it is in the late poems: more conscious because more directly selected and contrived and done as exercise; less conscious because there seemed a real identification between the speakers or personae of the poems and a world of myth, legend, and folk tale, and an implicit belief that metamorphosis of the self into a supernaturally heightened nature would in fact lead to a kind of rebirth. The later poems have a complex mythological framework which is far more integrated from poem to poem and within each poem. But the "fabulous" figures of the *Ariel* poems—the moon, the trees, vampires, stones, Lady Lazarus, the beehive and the queen bee—operate as a symbolic schema (though not anything so definite as an allegory) which mediates between self and world. They stand for possibilities of the self, and for descriptions of the world in which the self must move, and they represent certain choices the self has. The difference perhaps is between operating within a mythical schema on the one hand and on the other hand using that mythical schema to make a point about the relation between self and world. Thus Plath herself does not become mythic, as Robert Lowell and Edward Butscher have suggested.[46] She uses myth, adapting it to her own ends.

The image of the beehive is an example of how Plath makes the mythical intersect with the social in her late poems. Throughout the five bee poems in *Ariel*, Plath connects the metaphor of the beehive, with all its richly mythic allusions, to contemporary social and economic factors.

STASIS AND PROCESS:
THE BEEHIVE

The beehive [is] a perfect prototype of the first society, based on the gynocracy of motherhood. . . . The bee was rightly looked upon as the symbol of the feminine potency of nature. It was associated above all with Demeter, Artemis, and Persephone.

Erich Neumann, *The Great Mother*[47]

Plath's most promising attempt in *Ariel* at resolving the conflict between stasis and process, purity and rebirth, is her image of the beehive. The five bee poems in *Ariel*—"The Bee Meeting," "The Arrival of the Bee Box," "Stings," "The Swarm," and "Wintering"— written, in that order, between October 3 and October 9, 1962, contain one of Sylvia Plath's more complex statements of the tension between self-image and image of the world, Apollo and Dionysus, dying and living, the alienation or the integration of the individual into her society. They move beyond the retaliatory anger of "Daddy" to a vision of a female community with mutual work and survival interests.

The beehive is a complex image cluster which goes beyond itself to draw together a number of Plath's other major images: the moon, the tree, the stone. The image of the beehive makes a distinction between the functioning world of the hive, the female worker bees centered around their queen, and the essentially alien drones. Plath was familiar with Erich Neumann's *The Great Mother*, published in 1955, and her word choice in the bee poems in *Ariel* often echoes Neumann's. Kroll's *Chapters in a Mythology* includes a fascinating, lengthy, and specific discussion of Plath's use of Neumann and elements of the White Goddess myth in her poetry as moon/goddess/witch.[48] My own interest in these poems is in Plath's political use of mythical material. For, though the derivation of the bee imagery is mythical, Plath is careful to place the image of the beehive within a social context. She does this most systematically through the stages she traces in these poems of the relationship between the poet, the beehive, and the beekeeper. She moves from her father as beekeeper in the three pre-*Ariel* bee poems to an image of the village midwife as beekeeper and finally to herself as beekeeper in *Ariel*. Thus a complex set of identifications between the bees and herself and a complex set of oppositions between the bees and an essentially patriarchal human world is set up; also suggested are a number of ways in which the metaphor of the beehive relates to the larger context of a capitalist society.

Sylvia Plath's father, Otto Plath, a professor of biology at Boston University and a recognized authority on bees, published *Bumblebees and Their Ways* in 1934, two years after Sylvia was born. In three early poems—"Lament" (1951–52), "Electra on Azalea Path" (1959), and "The Beekeeper's Daughter" (1959)— Plath directs the symbolic significance of the bees and the beehive toward her relationship with her father. In "Lament," an awkward early poem, her father is described as a god-like figure oblivious to storm, sea and lightning, who was nevertheless and ludicrously struck down by a swarm of bees. "A scowl of sun struck down my mother, / tolling her grave with golden gongs, / but the sting of bees took away my father." By the time she writes the two 1959 poems, Plath has begun to identify herself with the bees and thus somehow to assign herself guilt for her father's death, even though she says, in the opening stanza of "Electra on Azalea Path," "I had nothing to do with guilt or anything." "Electra on Azalea Path" begins by identifying the speaker of the poem with a hive of wintering bees. "The day you died I went into the dirt / . . . Where bees, striped black and gold, sleep out the blizzard / Like hieratic stones," she says, and, "It was good for twenty years, that wintering—." Somehow, she implies in this poem, it was her birth that presaged her father's death, and her love which finally killed him. Her assumption of guilt is clear in the poem's end: "O pardon the one who knocks for pardon at / Your gate, father—your hound-bitch, daughter, friend. / It was my love that did us both to death."

Plath built up a mythical temporal schema into which she fit what she saw as the significant events in her life. Thus she says in "Lady Lazarus" of her suicide attempts, "I have done it again. / One year in every ten / I manage it—." Her first suicide attempt was at age twenty, during the summer of 1953, and she worked backward and forward from this center. She sometimes says she was ten when her father died, but actually she had just turned eight years old when he died on November 2, 1940. Her birthday is October 27, and her father was dying then, so it is not strange that an eight-year-old would connect the two events and feel a certain guilt. Especially since, as Plath suggests in a number of places, including "Electra on Azalea Path," her mother quite naturally tried to soften the loss to her children: "My mother said; you died like any man. / How shall I age into that state of mind?" To an eight-year-old child, who felt the loss of her father but didn't quite understand it, his disappearance followed by what might have seemed a conspiracy of silence would have been both strange and suspicious. Why was no one saying anything to her about her father? Was it because his death was somehow her fault?[49] In any case, Plath makes her father's death fall a third of the way through her life, and her own first suicide attempt marks the second third.

That her final and successful suicide attempt came at age thirty does suggest that to some extent she became caught up in her own systematizing. Of course, the actual reasons for seeing suicide as a solution go far beyond what some readers of Plath's poetry have been tempted to call a need to reenact in life what one has structured in art.

"The Beekeeper's Daughter" (*The Colossus*) is a description of a lush, symbolically female scene of open flowers, dense scented air, and "many-breasted hives." As a natural by-product of their food gathering, the bees are cross-fertilizing the flowers, and the entire poem has an intensely sexual atmosphere. The man, the beekeeper, moves through this rich, lush landscape, spare, vertical, and essentially alien to it. The one line in the poem that describes him is: "Hieratical in your frock coat, maestro of the bees." Her father, the beekeeper, is designated as priest-like; he both controls and sanctifies the riot of fertilization going on around him while remaining aloof from it himself. Speaking of the moon, a female image connected to that of the beehive, Neumann writes:

This patriarchal consciousness that says, "The victory of the male lies in the spiritual principle," devaluates the moon and the feminine element to which it belongs. It is "merely of the soul," "merely" the highest form of an earthly and material development that stands in opposition to the "pure spirit" that in its Apollonian-Platonic and Jewish-Christian form has led to the abstract conceptuality of modern consciousness. But this modern consciousness is threatening the existence of Western mankind, for the one-sidedness of masculine development has led to a hypertrophy of consciousness at the expense of the whole man.[50]

The speaker of this poem, the beekeeper's daughter, is, one might imagine, following along through the garden behind her father; her response to what is emotionally taking place is three lines, one of which follows each of the three stanzas: "My heart under your foot, sister of a stone"; "A fruit that's death to taste: dark flesh, dark parings"; and "The queen bee marries the winter of your year." The speaker of the poem functions primarily as an observer, watching both her father and the bees in the garden, but there are already the beginnings of an identification of the poet with the bees, especially with the queen bee, which characterizes the later bee poems in *Ariel*. Certainly the speaker of "The Bee-keeper's Daughter" sympathizes with the fertile atmosphere and activity of the garden and wants to convert to this type of response to the universe the one figure which is out of place: the beekeeper, frock-coated, probably in black, upright walking, and priest-like or celibate. It is also a way of sanctioning and mediating sexual desire for her long-dead father or for what he represents. Plath is quite aware of this as the title of the contemporaneous "Electra on Azalea Path" indicates.

The question of where the poet herself stands, in relation to the beekeeper's separation from the garden and in relation to the bees' natural functioning within it, is considered in great detail in the bee poems in *Ariel*. These five poems form a cycle of the stages of the hive and also a cycle of the relationship of the beekeeper to the hive and of the poet to the metaphor of the beehive. From the summer of 1961 through December 1962, while Sylvia Plath and Ted Hughes lived in a country house in Devon, Plath became an enthusiastic beekeeper. Given the impulse toward rebirth in Plath's poetry, it is significant for the bee poems in *Ariel* that the person who introduced her to beekeeping was the local midwife, who had assisted at the birth of Plath's second child.

What characterizes "The Bee Meeting" is its atmosphere of ritual. "The Beekeeper's Daughter" also had ritual elements, but the center of the poem was her father as beekeeper and outside herself, except insofar as the poem as a whole was a ritual. In "The Bee Meeting," the poet herself has taken over her father's role, has become the beekeeper, or is in the process of so doing. The poem is a rite of investiture. As a rite, it can be seen in at least three ways in this poem. First, she is being made a priest and dressed in priestly robes. Her relationship to the beehive in this sense is not so much as an actor or participant, but as a conductor of the action. She is also being initiated into a group of "priests," others robed as she is. Second, when they give her the "fashionable white straw Italian hat / And a black veil that moulds to my face," they are not only making her one of them, they are also to some extent setting her apart from them in their own "veils tacked to ancient hats," their "square black" heads. In some sense, she is being crowned, foreshadowing her fascination and finally identification with the queen bee, the still center of the hive. Third, the white crown the speaker of the poem receives is possibly a scape-goat's crown as well; that is, because of her quite understandable fear of the bees, she partly sees herself in the role of victim to them, a kind of living sacrifice in a pagan religion. So the investiture going on in the poem is simultaneously that of priest, god/queen, and sacrifice.

The last stanza of "The Bee Meeting," brings all of these possibilities together and begins Plath's identification with the bees:

> I am exhausted, I am exhausted—
> Pillar of white in a blackout of knives.
> I am the magician's girl who does not flinch.
> The villagers are untying their disguises, they are shaking hands.
> Whose is that long white box in the grove, what have they
>   accomplished,
>   why am I cold?

The white straw Italian hat and the white hive earlier in the poem, the magician's girl and the knife thrower's assistant who is a white pillar, and the white box in the last line which is both the beehive and the speaker's coffin, pull together the set of identifications within the poem. The exhaustion, the fear of death in the knife throwing image, and the coffin/hive equation also connect the bee poems to the theme of rebirth in *Ariel*. It is necessary to die to be reborn. The crucial question in *Ariel* is whether these symbolic deaths, these imaginative transformations of self, will ever lead to a rebirth into a transformed and positive world. The bee poems, taken as a whole, seem to be the only extended imaginative structure in Sylvia Plath's poetry which suggest that a transformation of self and world might occur together.

In both "The Bee Meeting" and "The Arrival of the Bee Box" the speaker of the poem is still separate from the bees. She has moved into what was originally her father's role, beekeeper, but she has not yet fully identified with the bees, though she is, in "The Bee Meeting," looking beyond the villagers to the bees themselves. The dominant emotion in these two poems is fear, fear that the bees will turn on her, drive her away, reject her. "The Bee Meeting" is one of Plath's rare poems ("Mushrooms" and "Daddy" are two others) where the speaker of the poem is in a community, part of a group engaged in a concerted action, though it is true that in "The Bee Meeting" her legitimacy as a member of this community (of beekeepers) is the subject of the poem and of much of her ambivalence.[51]

The possibility of a qualitatively different rebirth is central to the bee poems. In "The Arrival of the Bee Box," the hive is also conditionally and initially compared to a coffin. The crate full of bees is an intrusion, though she ordered it; it frightens her, though she reminds herself that she is the owner. Like death, the crate of bees repels and attracts her at the same time. "The box is locked, it is dangerous. / I have to live with it overnight / And I can't keep away from it." The poem is a series of fantasies based on the question: what shall I do with them? She can send them back; she can let them stay in the box and starve. Then she thinks, what if I let them out? What would happen?

> I wonder if they would forget me
> If I just undid the locks and stood back and turned into a tree.
> There is the laburnum, its blond colonnades,
> And the petticoats of the cherry.

The speaker of the poem imagines herself, like Daphne, turning into a tree to escape a threat. A follower of Artemis, goddess of the moon and of purity and chastity, Daphne was the unwilling object of Apollo's infatuation. Her allegiance to Artemis in danger, she appealed to her father, a minor river god, for help, and he turned her into a tree. Plath's use of this fable is revealing, and it suggests a number of possibilities for transformation. Apollo, the sun god, the oracle, and a patron of poetry and philosophy, represented to the Greeks who created him an intellectual, rational approach to life. Experience could be understood and controlled to some extent in language. Dionysus, the god of wine and fecundity, was the other side of classical Greek religion and philosophy. Also associated with poetry, Dionysus represented divine inspiration or creative frenzy and a sensual, organic approach to experience. With the Apollonian we associate intellectuality, the sun, and, as noted previously in Plath's poetry, depersonalization and sterility. Apollo is seen as representing an essentially patriarchal approach, the god of the ruling class. Dionysus or Bacchus, with his entourage of maddened women, represented sensuality, frenzy, darkness, fertility, and imagination; he was the god of a conquered culture. The latter is a combination which opens the individual to more danger because it requires commitment and involvement rather than separation. However, Dionysus also represents a loss of control and in that sense a loss of self. The captive bees in "The Arrival of the Bee Box" are described in Dionysian terms; they are "black on black," noisy, unintelligible, angry. The two alternatives the poet feels herself faced with are to identify with the bees or to identify with her father the beekeeper, thereby making the Apollonian choice of separation and intellectuality. In this poem, and perhaps finally in her poetry as a whole, Plath sidesteps this particular choice, or rather redefines it by choosing an allegiance to Artemis, by accepting the moon as her muse instead of either the rationality of Apollo or the uncontrolled frenzy of Dionysus.

In *The Goddess*, Christine Downing remarks:

Contemplation of Artemis's solitude provokes not only fear of loneliness but of savagery, wildness, of a passion entirely different from Aphrodite's sensual indulgence of feeling. In Artemis's realm, feelings do not issue in creative expression or in sexual involvement. One does not do anything with them; one simply comes to know them. . . . The very taming of feeling is beside the point. The feelings evoked in her realm are of many hues—vulnerability, solicitude, rage, instability. They include the painful sense of implacable otherness, and even the ache of not having access to one's deepest feelings. Each is pure, entire, for the time all-encompassing.

In Artemis, passion and virginity are strangely intertwined, as are the wildness and remoteness of her woodland habitat. Artemis and her wildness both invite and resist violation. We long, like Callisto, to enter "a woods that no one throughout the years has touched"; yet, once we have entered it, it is no longer a virgin forest. The wilderness becomes an ever-receding and even more fantasmal reality.[52]

Artemis is remote, like her twin brother Apollo. She is inviolable, often cold and cruel. She is associated with all the biological life stages of women—menstruation, birthing, menopause. "Before her marriage the girl takes her dolls and the clothes she has worn as a child and in propitiation dedicates them to Artemis."[53]

The search of Sylvia Plath's poetry for a transformed self reborn into a transformed world can be seen as a search for an androgynous self and world. The two extremes of Apollo and Dionysus are finally unsatisfactory for a woman poet precisely because both are male defined. Artemis, goddess of the moon and the forests, Artemis the huntress, protector of pregnant women and virgin goddess, is an androgynous choice, if only because of her essential self-sufficiency and transcendence of sexually based behavior patterns. Artemis represents androgyny defined from a female rather than a male perspective.[54] However, Cynthia Secor, in "Androgyny: An Early Reappraisal," suggests that the image of the androgyne is less useful for women than the image of the strong woman—for example, the witch or the Amazon—because while the latter suggest energy, power, and movement, the androgyne is an image of "static completion."[55] Static completion is one pole of the possibilities for self Plath works with in the late poems; she uses it most directly in poems like "Edge," where the moon invokes dormancy and sense deprivation, and the self is removed from passion and process.

Sylvia Plath's vacillation between Dionysian and Apollian modes of perception, her fascination with the moon, the tree, the stone, and the beehive, all traditionally connected mythic symbols for the original, undifferentiated primal Feminine which she places against traditional male-oriented symbols, reflect a need, on the part of the creative artist who is a woman, to transcend at the least the limiting manifestations of sex role differentiations and to reach some androgynous moment of aesthetic and mystical completion. Judith Kroll points out Plath's familiarity with Robert Graves's 1961 *Oxford Addresses on Poetry*; in "The Dedicated Poet," Artemisian and Dionysian qualities come together into what Graves calls the Muse.

Apollonian poetry is composed in the forepart of the mind: wittily, . . . always reasonably, always on a preconceived plan, and derived from a close knowledge of rhetoric, prosody, Classical example, and contemporary fashion. . . . The Apollonian allows no personal emotions to obtrude, and no unexpected incident to break the smooth, musical flow of his verse. The pleasure he offers is consciously aesthetic.

Muse poetry is composed at the back of the mind: an unaccountable product of a trance in which the emotions of love, fear, anger, or grief are profoundly engaged, though at the same time powerfully disciplined;

in which intuitive thought reigns supralogically, and personal rhythm subdues metre to its purposes. The effect on readers of Muse poetry, with its opposite poles of ecstasy and melancholia, is what the French call a *frisson*, and the Scots call a "grue"—meaning the shudder provoked by fearful or supernatural experiences."[56]

For the poet to turn into a tree, like Daphne, or to put on her "moon suit and funeral veil," as she does in "The Arrival of the Bee Box," is to make a mediating choice, for though Artemis is not identical to Graves's Muse, she is kin to her; Artemis is like Dionysus in her passion and wildness, and like Apollo in her austerity. And indeed, Plath's poetry combines a highly emotional, intense tone with a tightly controlled form. However, as the association of funeral veil with moon suit suggests, the possibility of an allegiance to Artemis is finally ambivalent as well, since her remoteness also implies, for Plath, not only invulnerability but separation, nonfertility, and death. The speaker of "The Arrival of the Bee Box" says at last, "I am no source of honey / So why should they turn on me?"

There is a connection between this fear of her own possible sterility in "The Arrival of the Bee Box" and the central theme of "The Swarm" (which she wrote a day after "Stings," but "Stings" and "Wintering" will be discussed together). One of Plath's war poems, like "Totem" and "Getting There," "The Swarm" describes the negative historical and economic context in which the positive myth of the beehive exists. "The Swarm" is perhaps the least successful poetically of the bee poems, perhaps because it is too cluttered; it tries to make too many connections that are not fully worked out within the poem. What is both interesting and clear about this poem, however, is the identification of Napoleon—and the beginning of modern warfare on a large and impersonal scale—with "the man with gray hands." Literally the bee seller, the man with gray hands represents competitive capitalism and the spirit of the modern industrial West.

> The man with gray hands smiles—
> The smile of a man of business, intensely practical.
> They are not hands at all
> But asbestos receptacles.

What the man of business does is to disrupt the cycle of nature for practical and mercenary ends. The poet, in her sympathy with the bees, sees them metaphorically as victims of war, their flight halted, "the honeycomb / Of their dream" shot down, defeated. As one who stands to profit from this interruption of nature's cycle, though, the speaker of the poem feels complicity. She is caught between the bees and the beeseller, between the victims of war and the warmakers. She is caught somewhere between the present system and some alternative, between forces that sustain the status quo and forces that question it.

The relationship between the poet and the bees is complex, ambivalent and deliberately ambiguous throughout the bee poems. She is somewhere in between the efficient humans like the beeseller who see in the bees only profit, and therefore remain separate from them as had her father in "The Beekeeper's Daughter," and the bees themselves with whose essentially feminine and cyclic world she gradually begins to identify within these five poems. Because of her very ambivalence, she feels vulnerable to the bees. She feels at times that she must turn into a tree or something in nature in order to be safe from them. In contrast, the beeseller and those like him are invulnerable, their hands asbestos; they are invulnerable precisely because they do not identify with the bees. They see the bees solely as items of profit, as producers of a commodity which they can sell as well as the bees themselves. And along with their invulnerability goes a certain insensitivity and numbness. They are like the cardboard men in the office in *Three Women*, like the business partners in "Death & Co."

There is an analogy between the way these men of business see the beehive as a commodity and the poem as commodity. The capitalist world view, which trains us to see processes as products, also transforms art into a commodity, to be marketed and sold and inventoried in the same way that the beehive and the honey are not a mystery but simply a commodity to the men with gray hands. What effect does the definition of art as commodity have on the artist, particularly on a woman poet unsure already of her identity and her place in a male tradition of poetry? It is significant that Sylvia Plath, undeniably one of the best American poets writing since the Second World War, began her career as a writer by training herself to produce stories which would sell to the popular magazines. This is not surprising, for in a capitalist economy, identity and worth are often validated by a cash payment. Plath's identification with the bees in these poems, particularly with the queen bee, the creative center of the hive, in opposition to the beeseller, is one way of stating the conflict between the creative artist and a capitalist bureaucratic society.

Beekeeping seems in these five poems to be as well a metaphor for the act of making poems, for the work of a poet, especially if one keeps in mind Robert Graves's distinction between Apollonian poetry and Muse poetry.[57] The bees' conversion of pollen to honey is essentially a mystery, as is the Muse poet's channel to the unconscious and its powerful images and emotions. Beekeeping itself is analagous to the application of poetic craft and discipline toward the shaping of raw material, though in another sense the poet/beekeeper is a midwife, like the woman who introduced Plath to beekeeping and helped deliver her second child. As midwife, the beekeeper/poet is primarily witness to and facilitator of a process of creation outside her conscious control. Whether to remain in control or to give up control is paralleled in these poems by the speaker's choice of whether to ally with the gray men with asbestos hands or with the bees themselves. A mediating choice is for the poet to gain control through giving up control, through accepting that the creative process itself, though in her, is outside her conscious control, though she can shape through craft what she is given to work with. In "Stings," it is her identification with the hive, her resolution at last of where her loyalties lie, that finally allows her to say: "I am in control. / Here is my honey-machine, / It will work without thinking."

Plath's closest identification of herself with the bees as woman and as poet is in "Wintering" and "Stings," which are concerned with the life cycle or stages of the hive. In "Wintering" the speaker of the poem feels guilty; she has "whirled the midwife's extractor" and taken their honey and now the bees must live through the winter on an artificial substitute. In her role as beekeeper, she feels as though she has exploited them. The fear which had been directed at the bees themselves in "The Arrival of the Bee Box" is in "Wintering" directed rather at the dark cellar she has put them in and in which she herself feels suffocated. She begins the poem as beekeeper presumably in control of the bees and their product, her six jars of honey, but by the fourth stanza the dynamic has reached its own conclusion and reversed: "Possession. / It is they who own me." With this giving up of ownership and control and her position as a woman of business, her fear also seems to disappear as her identification with the bees takes its place. In "Wintering," this identification remains generic rather than specific.

> The bees are all women,
> Maids and the long royal lady.
> They have got rid of the men,
>
> The blunt, clumsy stumblers, the boors.
> Winter is for women—
> The woman, still at her knitting,
> At the cradle of Spanish walnut

Endurance, waiting, a capacity to reduce life down to its essentials in order to survive are the qualities of the bees Plath focuses on in "Wintering." Plath ends "Wintering" with the spring flight of the bees and in "Stings," which marks the closest identification of the poet with the bees, she discusses characteristics of the hive which are corollaries to those in "Wintering": movement instead of stasis, rebirth instead of waiting, vengeance instead of endurance.

The hive exists as a colony, a society which can be seen from the outside as a single entity. In "The Bee Meeting," the poet sees the hive as a virgin, sealed off and inwardly brooding. But the hive has a center: the queen. Normally, the queen is the unmoving center of a vortex of activity of the worker bees, neutered females. She does not move unless the hive swarms. In the society of the beehive, the queen alone is capable of creativity and, though she will eventually be destroyed by a new queen, the hive itself has the potential for immortality. Neumann's discussion of the symbol of the beehive in *The Great Mother* is particularly helpful to a reading of "Stings."

The "virginity" of the Great Mother, i.e., her independence of the male, becomes particularly evident in the Amazonian bee state, where only the queen is fecundated by the male, and she only once. For this reason, and because of the food she eats, the bee is pure; Demeter must, like the

Vestals and many other priestesses of the Great Mother, be virgins. And among the bees, as so often among beasts and men, matriarchal womanhood assumes a character of the "terrible" in its relation to the males; for after mating, the drone mate and all other drones are slain like aliens by the female group inhabiting the hive.

The beehive is an attribute of the Great Goddess as Demeter-Ceres-Spes. But the bee is also associated with the moon: the priestesses of the moon goddess were called "bees," and it was believed that all honey came from the moon, the hive whose bees were the stars.[58]

The association of the bee with the moon, the use of and then independence from the male, the related concept of purity, and the "terrible" (a word Plath echoes in "Stings") vengeance of the bees, all are part of the complex of associations which adhere to Plath's image of the beehive. In "Stings," the poet has moved from a generic identification of the beehive as a female society to a specific exploration of her own identity in her differentiation of the queen bee and the worker bees.

There are three separate distinctions in the speaker's self-image in "Stings." The first, and perhaps least important for this poem, is the distinction between the bees and herself as beekeeper, though it is important to note that here, for the first time, she is not afraid of the bees: "Bare-handed, I hand the combs." The second distinction is between herself (both as beekeeper and therefore observer, and as the bees and therefore participant) and the third person whom the bees attack: "The bees found him out, / Molding onto his lips like lies, / Complicating his features."[59] Finally, and most important to this poem, there is the distinction between herself as worker bee and herself as queen bee. The first image is centered on the old queen and she asks of the hive: "Is there any queen at all in it?"

> If there is, she is old,
> Her wings torn shawls, her long body
> Rubbed of its plush—
> Poor and bare and unqueenly and even shameful.
> I stand in a column
>
> Of winged, unmiraculous women,
> Honey-drudgers.

> I am no drudge
> Though for years I have eaten dust
> And dried plates with my dense hair.

The two roles Plath has been playing—as wife, mother, hostess, and secretary on the one hand and as poet on the other—correspond in many ways to these two images of the workers and the queen bee. She says in a letter written early in her marriage that she is going to manage all of these at once, but there must have been a fairly constant worry about whether she could and about whether the noncreative roles which take up so much time in a woman's life would drain from the artist her creativity. The roles of wife, mother, hostess, secretary define essentially static tasks, since the activity is cyclical and soon undone. A clean house is dirtied, a meal is consumed, your husband's latest poems are typed, and the same chores start over again the next day. One of the first signs of Esther Greenwood's "madness" in *The Bell Jar* is her refusal to wash her clothes or hair, since she'll just have to do it all over again the next day.[60] The work produced by the artist is different in kind from that produced by the roles a woman is traditionally expected to assume.

The last two stanzas of "Stings," after the worker bees have turned on the third person, exposed him and sent him away, are of the flight of the queen, reborn into solitude and creativity.

> They thought death was worth it, but I
> Have a self to recover, a queen.
> Is she dead, is she sleeping?
> Where has she been,
> With her lion-red body, her wings of glass?
>
> Now she is flying
> More terrible than she ever was, red
> Scar in the sky, red comet
> Over the engine that killed her—
> The mausoleum, the wax house.

These two images, of the old and reborn queen, correspond to the two self-images of "Lady Lazarus," a poem which is also about the relation between the poet and a society which consistently defines her in a way she feels to be false. Like the arrow into the red eye of morning in "Ariel," like Lady Lazarus, who rises out of the ash with her red hair, the queen is reborn. Her flight is an escape, a defiance, and an act of creation all at once, since this is literally the beginning of a new cycle and a new hive. In general, Plath is more interested in the beginnings and endings, the crisis points, of the cycle, than in its quiescent periods. She is interested in potential transformations of self.

However, what works against transformation of self are the internalized conflicts of identity within the poet. There are two separate conflicts of identity within the bee poems and they finally work against each other. First is the conflict between bee and beekeeper. The self-image as bee, with its associations of periodic rebirth and the sense of being an integral part of a community, of purity and wholeness, of a connection not only with one's immediate society but with a larger, transcendent world, moves the poet toward an androgynous moment of completion, union, and dialectical cyclical alternation of stasis and process. On the other hand is her self-image as beekeeper, modeled on the intellectuality of her father, an exploiter of the bees, manipulator of them, interrupter and interpreter of their cycle but separate from them, like the man of business with asbestos hands. This particular conflict occurs in various forms throughout Plath's late poetry—in the conflict between poet and audience in "Lady Lazarus," in "Daddy" in the conflict between a patriarchal authority structure and the woman who speaks the poem, in "Tulips" between health and illness, presence and absence.

The second conflict of identity becomes explicit in "Stings" in the two images of herself as worker and as queen.

> I am no drudge
> Though for years I have eaten dust
> And dried plates with my dense hair.
>
> And seen my strangeness evaporate,
> Blue dew from dangerous skin.
> Will they hate me,
> These women who only scurry,
> Whose news is the open cherry, the open clover?

This need to set the creative part of herself, the poet, off from the drudge who does "women's work," and to see her poetic self as both strange and dangerous, is one way of resolving a central dilemma of the woman artist. Which of the two women am I: the one who feels driven by the need to create, who can say "the blood jet is poetry, / There is no stopping it," or the woman who does work which no one takes seriously, least of all herself? What this conflict can lead to is a contempt for other women and for that aspect of herself which she sees as "drudge."

In fact, Sylvia Plath had little real contact with other women. Esther Greenwood's rejection of one unsatisfactory female role model after another—from Dorene to J. C. to her mother—in *The Bell Jar* is indicative. In particular, Plath had very little contact with other women writers. Though she got to know Anne Sexton slightly when they both sat in on Robert Lowell's poetry class one summer, though she writes in a letter to her brother how excited she is finally to have met Adrienne Rich, describing her as "the girl whose poetry I've followed from her first publication," Plath seemed to have very little sense of a community among women writers based on similar interests and themes.[61] Like most of the handful of women poets successful in the first two-thirds of the twentieth century, Sylvia Plath aligned herself primarily with male poets. To identify oneself as a woman poet, a poetess, was to admit that you did not expect to be taken seriously. Even the most cursory survey of American literary criticism yields examples of negative and patronizing pronouncements based on the poet or novelist's sex.[62] Yet the themes of Plath's strongest poetry are clearly based on her experience as a woman poet trying to do creative work in a field which had been overwhelmingly male-dominated and in a world which did not take women's creativity seriously. The lack of community among women writers in the 1950s and early 1960s had, for Plath, the result of isolating her within her own psyche. If any one thing leads to Sylvia Plath's anger and her sense, finally, that there was no place to get to, it is this experience of isolation: temporally, from history, in that she could not find a tradition from which she did not feel alienated; spatially, in that she could not find a community that shared her language, images, assumptions.

This experience of isolation is connected, for a woman writer, to ambivalence about self-image, image of the world, and relationship between self and world: an ambivalence that arises from being defined not by oneself, but by some other, and from being defined in a way that provides little support for creative and committed action on the part of the individual so defined. Sylvia Plath's attempt, from *The Colossus* poems on, to redefine herself through a medium, language, of which she is suspicious, her uneasiness that language is based on social expectations and assumptions shaped by an economic base and a cultural superstructure inimical to her own growth, create an ambivalence that leads to a kind of existential paralysis, a sense that one is enclosed in a circumscribed and solitary place where no real choice is possible.[63]

Even the metaphor of the beehive, Plath's most positive image of the possibility of community, is finally ambivalent. The self is both bee and beekeeper, worker and queen, on the boundary between commitment and alienation, trapped within her culture but refusing to accept her assigned place in it. Sylvia Plath's poetry images and narrates the various forms that the conflict of self and world within the self can take. To see yourself trapped between sets of mutually exclusive alternatives, neither of which fits no matter how many reconciling images you generate, is to live in a circus hall of mirrors, where the self is distorted, disguised, or shattered into slivers of reflection. But it is the struggle to be whole that engages the poet and empowers the poems.

NOTES

1. Ted Hughes remarks, however, that Plath's

> poetic strategies, the poetic events she draws out of her experience of disintegration and renewal, the radiant visionary light in which she encounters her family and the realities of her daily life, are quite different in kind from anything one finds in Robert Lowell's poetry, or Anne Sexton's. Their work is truly autobiographical and personal. . . . The autobiographical details in Sylvia Plath's poetry work differently. She sets them out like masks, which are then lifted up by dramatis personae of nearly supernatural qualities.

"Notes on the Chronological Order of Sylvia Plath's Poems," *Tri-Quarterly*, no. 7 (Fall 1966), p. 81.

2. Ted Hughes dates the third and final phase of Sylvia Plath's work from about September 1960 until her death on February 11, 1963 [intro-

duction to *The Collected Poems*, p. 17]. I agree with Jon Rosenblatt and others that in general it makes sense to divide that period further into transitional poetry (1960–61, including most of the poems of *Crossing the Water*) and late poetry (1962–63, encompassing most of the poems in *Ariel* and *Winter Trees*, including the radio play, "Three Women"). [Rosenblatt, *Sylvia Plath: The Poetry of Initiation*, p. 87.] This neat division does break down at points, however, in that a poem like "Tulips" (March 18, 1961) is thematically and formally more a "late" poem than transitional.

3. Kroll, *Chapters in a Mythology: The Poetry of Sylvia Plath*, passim.

4. For a more extended discussion of this point, see Margaret Atwood, *Survival: A Thematic Guide to Canadian Literature* (Toronto: Anansi, 1972); Kate Ellis, "Women, Culture, and Revolution" in *Radical Teacher*, no. 2 (1976), pp. 3–8; Arnold Rampersad, "The Ethnic Voice in American Poetry," in *San Jose Studies* 2, no. 3 (November 1976), pp. 26–36; Barbara Charlesworth Gelpi, "A Common Language: The American Woman Poet" in *Shakespeare's Sisters: Feminist Essays on Women Poets*, eds., Sandra M. Gilbert and Susan Gubar (Bloomington: Indiana University Press, 1979), pp. 269–79, Pamela J. Annas, "A Poetry of Survival: Unnaming and Renaming in the Poetry of Audre Lorde, Pat Parker, Sylvia Plath and Adrienne Rich" in *Colby Library Quarterly* 18, no. 1 (March 1982), pp. 9–25.

5. Georg Lukács, "The Intellectual Physiognomy in Characterization" in *Writer and Critic* (New York: Grosset and Dunlap, 1970), p. 151.

6. Friedan, *The Feminine Mystique*. See Chapter 12, "Progressive Dehumanization: The Comfortable Concentration Camp," pp. 271–98.

7. Stu Ewen, "Advertising as a Way of Life" in *Liberation* (January 1975), pp. 17–34.

8. *Letters Home*, p. 176 and passim.

9. For a thorough joint discussion of the poetry of Sylvia Plath and Ted Hughes, see Uroff, *Sylvia Plath and Ted Hughes*.

10. Ted Hughes, *Crow* (London: Faber and Faber, 1970) and *Wodwo* (London: Faber and Faber, 1967).

11. Ellmann, *Thinking About Women*, p. 171.

12. Woolf, *A Room of One's Own*, p. 54.

13. "The Social Context" was originally published in slightly different form as "The Self in the World: The Social Context of Sylvia Plath's Late Poems" in *Women's Studies: An Interdisciplinary Journal*, 7, nos. 1/2 (Winter 1980), pp. 171–83. Reprinted in Linda Wagner, ed., *Critical Essays on Sylvia Plath* (Boston: L. K. Hall, 1984), pp. 130–39.

14. Ken Kesey, *One Flew Over the Cuckoo's Nest* (New York: Viking Press, 1962), p. 38.

15. Introducing this poem in a reading prepared for BBC radio, Sylvia Plath commented: "In this poem, . . . the speaker is an executive, a sort of exacting super-salesman. He wants to be sure the applicant for his marvelous product really needs it and will treat it right." Quoted in *The Collected Poems*, p. 293. Whether we see the actors in this poem as salesman/buyer, interviewer/job applicant, or, as a colleague of mine suggested, welfare office/applicant, what is clear is the bureaucratic, capitalistic context.

16. Frederick Engels, *The Origin of the Family, Private Property and the State* (New York: International Publishers, 1942):

> The modern individual family is founded on the open or concealed domestic slavery of the wife, and modern society is a mass composed of these individual families as its molecules.
>
> In the great majority of cases today, at least in the possessing classes, the husband is obliged to earn a living and support his family, and that in itself gives him a position of supremacy without any need for special legal titles and privileges. *Within the family he is the bourgeois, and the wife represents the proletariat* (p. 37, italics mine).

17. The progress of monopoly capitalism in the twentieth century has, however, served to proletarianize people who thought (or whose parents thought) they had escaped from the working class—clericals, sales, and lower and middle management—and is now beginning to make workers, in the traditional sense of people who have to sell their labor piecemeal and who have no relation to or control over the product of their labor, out of the professional classes. See especially Parts 4 and 5, "The Growing Working Class Occupations" and "The Working Class," in Harry Braverman, *Labor and Monopoly Capital: The Degradation of Work in the Twentieth Century* (New York: Monthly Review Press, 1974), pp. 293–449.

18. Fredric Jameson, *Marxism and Form* (Princeton, N.J.: Princeton University Press, 1971), pp. 186–87.

19. W.E.B. DuBois, "The Souls of Black Folk" in *Three Negro Classics* (1903; rpt. New York: Avon, 1965), pp. 214–15.

20. Sylvia Plath, "Johnny Panic and the Bible of Dreams," in *Sylvia Plath: Johnny Panic and The Bible of Dreams/Short Stories, Prose, and Diary Excerpts* (New York: Harper & Row, 1978), pp. 153, 159. First published in *Atlantic* (September 1968), pp. 54–60.

21. Theodore Roethke, *Words for the Wind* (New York: Doubleday, 1955).

22. Friedan, *The Feminine Mystique*, p. 16.

23. Lévi-Strauss, *The Savage Mind*, pp. 23–24.

24. Rosenstein, "Reconsidering Sylvia Plath," pp. 44–51, 96–99.

25. Quoted in Lois Ames, "Notes Toward a Biography" in Charles Newman, ed., *The Art of Sylvia Plath*, p. 171.

26. Plath, "Johnny Panic and the Bible of Dreams," p. 302.

27. Ibid., pp. 302–3.

28. Quoted in M. L. Rosenthal, *The New Poets* (New York: Oxford University Press, 1967), p. 82.

29. Kroll, *Chapters in a Mythology*, p. 145.

30. Letter to Richard Sassoon, November 22, 1955. *The Journals of Sylvia Plath*, eds., Ted Hughes and Frances McCullough (New York: Dial Press, 1982), p. 91.

31. Sylvia Plath, "The Mother's Union" in *McCall's* (October 1972), pp. 81, 142. Reprinted as "The Mothers" in *Johnny Panic and the Bible of Dreams*, pp. 10, 19.

32. Perloff, *The Poetic Art of Robert Lowell*, pp. 179–84. Rosenblatt, *Sylvia Plath: The Poetry of Initiation*, passim.

33. Laing, *The Divided Self*, p. 45.

34. Ted Hughes, "Notes on the Chronological Order of Sylvia Plath's Poems," p. 195.

35. Robert Graves, *The White Goddess* (New York: Creative Age Press, 1948), p. 376. My discussion of *The Tempest* in this chapter was suggested by Anthony Libby's article "God's Lioness and the Priest of Sycorax: Plath and Hughes," in *Contemporary Literature* 15 (1974), pp. 386–405.

36. Denise Levertov, "Life at War" in *Poems 1960–1967* (New York: New Directions, 1983).

37. Ihab Hassan, *Contemporary American Literature, 1945–1972* (New York: Frederick Ungar Publishing Co., 1973), p. 133.

38. William Butler Yeats, "Sailing to Byzantium" in *The Collected Poems of William Butler Yeats* (New York: Macmillan, 1933).

39. Richard Wright, *Native Son* (New York: Harper and Row, 1940), pp. 391–92. Also interesting in this context is Hegel's discussion of the primacy of the act in *The Phenomenology of Mind*, trans., J. B. Baillie (New York: Macmillan, 1949), p. 350. Finally, he writes, "The individual human being *is* what the act *is*."

40. A. Alvarez, "Sylvia Plath," in *The Art of Sylvia Plath*, p. 65.

41. See Wilhelm Reich's *The Mass Psychology of Fascism* (New York: Simon and Schuster, 1969), particularly his chapter on "The Authoritarian Personality," for an analysis of how an oppressed class can contribute to its own oppression. Judith Lewis Herman, in *Father-Daughter Incest*

(Cambridge, Mass.: Harvard University Press, 1981), discusses the history of the suppression of incest beginning with Freud and continuing into contemporary psychological literature, the attribution of reports of incest to hysterical female oedipal fantasizing or, when the fact of incest is impossible to deny, assigning blame to the victim: what Herman calls the Seductive Daughter and/or the Collusive Mother (Chapter 1, "A Common Occurence"). Writing in the early 1960s and familiar with some of these attitudes, it is not surprising that Plath assigns some culpability to the victim. Herman goes on to say, "Even when the girl does give up her erotic attachment to her father, she is encouraged to persist in the fantasy that some other man, like her father, will some day take possession of her, raising her above the common lot of womankind" (p. 57).

I am not of course suggesting that Plath literally had an incestuous relationship with her father—there is no evidence one way or the other—but she does make recurrent use of father/daughter incest as a symbol for male/female relations in a patriarchal society. Herman's profile of the father who is an incest offender comes close to what is known about Otto Plath: such men are perfect patriarchs with absolute authority in their families who impress outsiders (and frequently their daughters) as sympathetic, admirable men. They are hardworking, good providers, who impose a strict sexual division of labor on their families, think women are inferior to men, and prefer sons to daughters. Frequently they are violent, using physical or psychological force to intimidate their families. The man who is most likely to commit father/daughter incest, concludes Judith Herman, is simply an intensified version of a "normal" man. (See Chapter 5, "Incestuous Fathers and Their Families.")

42. This photograph of Otto Plath is reproduced on page 17 of *Letters Home*.

43. Ellmann, *Thinking About Women*, pp. 119–23.

44. Quoted in Rosenthal, *The New Poets*, p. 82.

45. Graves, *The White Goddess*, p. 391.

46. Robert Lowell, in the preface to *Ariel*, writes that she is "hardly a person at all, or a woman, certainly not another 'poetess,' but one of those super-real, hypnotic, great classical heroines" (p. vii); Edward Butscher, in *Sylvia Plath: Method and Madness*, labels her "a bitch goddess."

47. Erich Neumann, *The Great Mother* (Princeton, N.J.: Princeton University Press, 1955), p. 265.

48. Kroll, *Chapters in a Mythology*, pp. 39–43 and passim.

49. In 1954 Plath described to a friend her reaction to her father's death. "He was an autocrat. I adored and despised him, and I probably wished many times that he were dead. When he obliged me and died, I imagined

that I had killed him." Quoted in Nancy Hunter Steiner, *A Closer Look at Ariel: A Memory of Sylvia Plath* (New York: Harper's Magazine Press, 1973), p. 45.

50. Neumann, *The Great Mother*, p. 57.

51. Judith Kroll, focusing on the speaker's attitude toward the queen bee and the virgins whom the villagers are removing (presumably to begin new hives), sees the villagers as interrupting a sacred ritual, a duel to the death out of which the hive would be revitalized and reborn: the queen is dead; long live the queen.

52. Cristine Downing, *The Goddess: Mythological Images of the Feminine* (New York: Crossroad, 1981), p. 173.

53. Ibid.

54. A more extended version of this discussion of androgyny appears in Pamela Annas, "New Worlds, New Words: Androgyny in Feminist Science Fiction," *Science Fiction Studies* 5, no. 15 (July 1978).

55. Cynthia Secor, "Androgyny: An Early Reappraisal," *Women's Studies: An Interdisciplinary Journal* 2 (1974), p. 165.

56. Robert Graves, *Oxford Addresses on Poetry* (New York: Doubleday, 1962), pp. 19–20.

57. See Carol Ferrier, "The Beekeeper's Apprentice" in Gary Lane, ed., *Sylvia Plath: New Views on the Poetry* (Baltimore: Johns Hopkins University Press, 1979), pp. 203–17. Ferrier is one of the few Plath critics who have discussed the political dimensions of Plath's poetry.

58. Neumann, *The Great Mother*, p. 267.

59. "Stings" was written at a time when Sylvia Plath's marriage to Ted Hughes was breaking up, and in a letter written about this time to her mother, Plath discussed the necessity for eschewing illusion and seeing her own world as it really was:

> Don't talk to me about the world needing cheerful stuff! What the person out of Belsen—physical or psychological—wants is nobody saying the birdies still go tweet-tweet, but the full knowledge that somebody else has been there and knows the *worst*, just what it is like. It is much more help for me, for example, to know that people are divorced and go through hell, than to hear about happy marriages. Let *The Ladies' Home Journal* blither about *those*.

(*Letters Home*, p. 124.)

60. Plath, *The Bell Jar*, pp. 104–5.

61. *Letters Home*, p. 339.

62. Mary Ellmann does a fairly thorough survey in *Thinking About Women*. Also see John Fekete, "The New Criticism," in *Telos*, no. 20 (Summer 1974), pp. 27–28, footnote 105.

63. Ingrid Lorch Turner, unpublished article, "Existential Paralysis in Women." Turner writes: "Uncertainty concerning who one is and what the world is like is bound to pervade an individual's experience when that individual lives a number of different roles simultaneously" (p. 6).

✦ Bibliography ✦

Aird, Eileen M. " 'Poem For a Birthday' to 'Three Women': Develop-
ment in the Poetry of Sylvia Plath." *Critical Quarterly* 24, no. 4
(1979): 63-72.
———. *Sylvia Plath: Her Life and Work.* Edinburgh: Oliver and Boyd,
1973; New York: Harper & Row, 1975.
———. "Variants in a Tape Recording of Fifteen Poems by Sylvia Plath."
Notes and Queries 19 (February 1972): 59-61.
Alexander, Paul, ed. *Ariel Ascending: Writings About Sylvia Plath.* New
York: Harper & Row, 1985.
Alvarez, Alfred. "The Art of Suicide." *Partisan Review* 37 (1970): 339-58.
———. "Sylvia Plath: The Cambridge Collection." *Cambridge Review* 90
(February 1969): 246-47.
———. "Sylvia Plath: A Memoir." *The Savage God: A Study of Suicide*,
3-42. London: Wiedenfeld and Nicholson, 1971; New York: Ran-
dom House, 1972.
Ames, Lois. "Notes Toward a Biography." In *The Art of Sylvia Plath*,
edited by Charles Newman, 155-73. Bloomington: Indiana Uni-
versity Press, 1970; London: Faber & Faber, 1970.
Annas, Pamela J. "The Self in the World: The Social Context of Sylvia
Plath's Late Poems." *Women's Studies: An Interdisciplinary Journal* 7,
no. 1/2 (1980): 171-83.
Ashford, Deborah. "Sylvia Plath's Poetry: A Complex of Irreconcilable
Antagonisms." *Concerning Poetry* 7, no. 1 (1974): 62-69.

Axelrod, Stevens Gould. "Plath's and Lowell's Last Words." *Pacific Coast Philology* 11 (1976): 5-74.

Bagg, Robert. "The Rise of Lady Lazarus." *Mosaic* 2 (Summer 1969): 9-36.

Balitas, Vincent D. "On Becoming a Witch: A Reading of Sylvia Plath's 'Witch Burning.' " *Studies in the Humanities* 4 (February 1975): 27-30.

Barnard, Caroline K. *Sylvia Plath*. Boston: Twayne Publishers, 1978.

Beirne, Daniel J. "Plath's 'Two Campers in Cloud Country.' " *Explicator* 42 (Fall 1983): 61-62.

Berman, Jeffrey. "Sylvia Plath and the Art of Dying: Sylvia Plath (1932-1963)." *University of Hartford Studies in Literature* 10 (1978): 137-55.

Boyers, Robert. "On Sylvia Plath." *Salmagundi* 21 (1973): 96-104.

———. "Sylvia Plath: The Trepanned Veteran." *Centennial Review* 13 (1969): 138-53.

Brink, Andrew. "Sylvia Plath and the Art of Redemption." *Alphabet* 15 (December 1968): 48-69.

Broe, Mary Lynn. "A Subtle Psychic Bond: Sylvia and Aurelia Schober Plath in *Letters Home*." In *The Lost Tradition: A History of Mothers and Daughters in Literature*, 217-30, edited by Esther Broner and Cathy Davidson. New York: Frederick Ungar, 1980.

———. "Demythologizing Sivvy: That 'Theatrical Comeback in Broad Day,' " *Poet and Critic* 10, no. 1 (1977): 30-39.

———. " 'Oh Dad, Poor Dad': Sylvia Plath's Comic Exorcism." *Notes on Contemporary Literature* 9, no. 4 (1979): 2-4.

———. "Recovering the Complex Self: Sylvia Plath's Beeline." *Centennial Review* 24 (Winter 1980): 1-24.

———. *Protean Poetic: The Poetry of Sylvia Plath*. Columbia, Mo.: University of Missouri Press, 1980.

Buell, Frederick. "Sylvia Plath's Traditionalism." *Boundary* 2 (Fall 1976): 195-211.

Burnham, Richard E. "Sylvia Plath's 'Lady Lazarus.' " *Contemporary Poetry* 1 (1973): 42-46.

Burton, Deirdre. "Through Glass Darkly: Through Dark Glasses: On Stylistic and Political Commitment—via a Study of a Passage from Sylvia Plath's *The Bell Jar*." In *Language and Literature: An Introductory Reader in Stylistics*, edited by Ronald Carter. London: Allen and Unwin, 1982, 195-214.

Butscher, Edward. *Sylvia Plath: Method and Madness*. New York: Seabury Press, 1976.

———, ed. *Sylvia Plath: The Woman and the Work*. New York: Dodd, 1977.

Campbell, Wendy. "Remembering Sylvia." In *The Art of Sylvia Plath*, edited by Charles Newman, 182-86. Bloomington: Indiana University Press, 1970; London Faber & Faber, 1970.

Caraher, Brian. "The Problematic of Body and Language in Sylvia Plath's 'Tulips.' " *Paunch* 42 (December 1975): 76-89.

Claire, William F. "That Rare, Random Descent: The Poetry and Pathos of Sylvia Plath." *Antioch Review* 26 (Winter 1966): 522-60.

Cleverdon, Douglas. "On 'Three Women.' " In *The Art of Sylvia Plath*, edited by Charles Newman, 227-29. Bloomington: Indiana University Press, 1970; London: Faber & Faber, 1970.

Cooley, Peter. "Autism, Autoeroticism, Auto-da-fé: The Tragic Poetry of Sylvia Plath." *Hollins Critic* 10 (February 1973): 1-15.

Corrigan, Sylvia Robinson. "Sylvia Plath: A New Feminist Approach." *Aphra* 1 (Spring 1970): 16-23.

Davis, Robin Reed. "Now I Have Lost Myself: A Reading of Sylvia Plath's 'Tulips.' " *Paunch* 42 (December 1975): 97-104.

Davison, Peter. "Inhabited by a Cry: The Last Poetry of Sylvia Plath." *Atlantic* (August 1966): 76-77.

Dickie, Margaret. "Sylvia Plath's Narrative Strategies." *Iowa Review* 13 (Spring 1982): 1-14.

———. *Sylvia Plath and Ted Hughes*. Urbana: University of Illinois Press, 1979.

Dobbs, Jeannine. " 'Viciousness in the Kitchen': Sylvia Plath's Domestic Poetry." *Modern Language Studies* 7 (Fall 1977): 11-25.

Donovan, Josephine. "Sexual Politics in Sylvia Plath's Short Stories." *Minnesota Review* 4 (Spring/Summer 1973): 150-57.

Doran, Rachel S. "Female—or Feminist: The Tension of Duality of Sylvia Plath." *Transition* 1 (1977/78): 14-20.

Dunn, Douglas. "Damaged Instruments." *Encounter* 37 (August 1971): 68-74.

Dyroff, Jan M. "Sylvia Plath: Perceptions in *Crossing the Water*." *Art and Literature Review* 1 (1972): 49-50.

Efron, Arthur. "Sylvia Plath's 'Tulips' and Literary Criticism." *Paunch* 42 (December 1975): 69-75.

———. " 'Tulips': Text and Assumptions." *Paunch* 42 (December 1975): 110-22.

Ellmann, Mary. "*The Bell Jar*: An American Girlhood." In *The Art of Sylvia Plath*, 221-26. Bloomington: Indiana University Press, 1970; London: Faber & Faber, 1970.

Eriksson, Pamela D. "Some Thoughts on Sylvia Plath." *Unisa English Studies* 10 (1972): 44-52.

Ferrier, Carole. "The Beekeeper and the Queen Bee." *Refractory Girl* (Spring 1973): 31-36.

Fraser, G. S. "A Hard Nut to Crack from Sylvia Plath." *Contemporary Poetry* 1 (Spring 1973): 1-12.

Gilbert, Deborah. "Transformations in 'Nick and the Candlestick.' " *Contemporary Poetry* 12 (1979): 29-32.

Gilbert, Sandra. "In Yeats' House: The Death and Resurrection of Sylvia Plath." In *Critical Essays on Sylvia Plath*, edited by Linda Wagner, 204-22. Boston: G. K. Hall, 1984.

———. " 'A Fine White Flying Myth': Confessions of a Plath Addict." *Massachusetts Review* 19 (1978): 585-603.

———. "Contemporary Poetry: Metaphors and Morals." *Contemporary Literature* 20 (1979): 116-23.

———. "Teaching Plath's 'Daddy' to Speak to Undergraduates." *Bulletin of the Association of Departments of English* 76 (Winter 1983): 38-42.

Giles, Richard F. "Plath's 'Maudlin.' " *Explicator* 40 (Spring 1982): 56-59.

Gordon, Jan B. " 'Who is Sylvia?' The Art of Sylvia Plath." *Modern Poetry Studies* 1 (170): 6-34.

Guttenberg, Barnett. "Sylvia Plath, Myth, and 'The Hanging Man.' " *Contemporary Poetry* 3 (1977): 17-23.

Hakeem, A. "Sylvia Plath's 'Elm' and Munch's 'The Scream.' " *English Studies* 55 (December 1974): 531-37.

Hardwick, Elizabeth. "Sylvia Plath." In *Seduction and Betrayal: Women and Literature*, edited by Elizabeth Hardwick, 104-24. New York: Random House, 1970.

Hardy, Barbara. "The Poetry of Sylvia Plath: Enlargement or Derangement?" *The Survival of Poetry: A Contemporary Survey*, edited by Martin Dodsworth, 164-92. London: Faber & Faber, 1970.

Herman, Judith B. "Plath's 'Daddy' and the Myth of Tereus and Philomela." *Notes on Contemporary Literature* 7 (1977): 9-10.

———. "Reflections on a Kitchen Table: A Note on Sylvia Plath's 'Black Rook in Rainy Weather.' " *Notes on Contemporary Literature* 7 (1977): 5.

Higgins, Judith. "Sylvia Plath's Growing Popularity with College Students." *University: A Princeton Quarterly* 58 (Fall 1973): 4-8; 28-33.

Himelick, Raymond. "Notes on the Care and Feeding of Nightmares: Burton, Erasmus, and Sylvia Plath." *Western Humanities Review* 28 (Autumn 1974): 313-26.

Hoffman, Nancy J. "Reading Women's Poetry: The Meaning and Our Lives." *College English* 34 (1972): 48-62.

Holbrook, David. "R. D. Laing and the Death Circuit." *Encounter* 31 (August 1968): 35-45.

————. *Sylvia Plath: Poetry and Existence*. London: Athlone Press, 1976.

Hosbaum, Philip. "The Temptations of Giant Despair." *Hudson Review* 25 (Winter 1972/73): 597-612.

Howe, Irving. "Sylvia Plath: A Partial Disagreement." *Harper's Magazine* (January 1972): 88-91.

Howes, Barbara. "A Note on *Ariel*." *Massachusetts Review* 8 (Winter 1967): 225-26.

Hoyle, James F. "Sylvia Plath: A Poetry of Suicidal Mania." *Literature and Psychology* 18 (1968): 187-203.

Hughes, Ted. "Notes on the Chronological Order of Sylvia Plath's Poems." In *The Art of Sylvia Plath*, edited by Charles Newman, 187-95. Bloomington: Indiana University Press, 1970; London: Faber & Faber, 1970.

————. "Sylvia Plath's *Crossing the Water*: Some Reflections." *Critical Quarterly* 13 (Summer 1971): 165-72.

Jackson, Laura (Riding). "Suitable Criticism." *University of Toronto Quarterly* 47 (1977): 74-85.

Jones, A. R. "Necessity and Freedom: The Poetry of Robert Lowell, Sylvia Plath, and Anne Sexton." *Critical Quarterly* 7 (Spring 1965): 11-30.

————. "On 'Daddy.'" In *The Art of Sylvia Plath*, edited by Charles Newman, 230-36. Bloomington: Indiana University Press; London: Faber & Faber, 1970.

Juhasz, Suzanne. " 'The Blood Jet': The Poetry of Sylvia Plath." In *Naked and Fiery Forms: Modern American Poetry by Women: A New Tradition*, edited by Suzanne Juhasz, 85-116. New York: Harper & Row, 1976.

Kloss, Robert J. "Further Reflections on Plath's Mirror." *University of Hartford Studies in Literature* 14 (1982): 11-22.

Kroll, Judith. *Chapters in a Mythology: The Poetry of Sylvia Plath*. New York: Harper & Row, 1976.

Krook, Dorothea. "Recollections of Sylvia Plath." *Critical Quarterly* 18 (1976): 5-14.

Lameyer, Gordon. "Sylvia at Smith." *Sylvia Plath: The Woman and the Work*, edited by Edward Butscher, 32-41. New York: Dodd, 1977.

Lane, Gary. "Sylvia Plath's 'The Hanging Man': A Further Note." *Contemporary Poetry* 2 (Spring 1975): 40-43.

————, ed. *Sylvia Plath: New Views on the Poetry*. Baltimore: Johns Hopkins University Press, 1979.

Lane, Gary, and Maria Stevens. *Sylvia Plath: A Bibliography*. Metuchen, N.J.: Scarecrow Press, 1978.

Lavers, Annette. "The World as Icon: On Sylvia Plath's Themes." In *The*

Art of Sylvia Plath, edited by Charles Newman, 1-135. Bloomington: Indiana University Press, 1970; London, Faber & Faber, 1970.

Lerner, Lawrence. "Review of *The Collected Poems*," *Encounter* 58 (January 1982), 53-54.

Libby, Anthony. "God's Lioness and the Priest of Sycorax: Plath and
Hughes." *Contemporary Literature* 15 (Summer 1974): 386-405.

Lindberg-Seyersted, Brita. "Notes on Three Poems by Sylvia Plath." *Edda*
74 (1974): 47-54.

————. "On Sylvia Plath's Poetry." *Edda* 72 (1972): 54-59.

Lowell, Robert. "Introduction" to *Ariel*. New York: Harper & Row,
1966.

Lucie-Smith, Edward. "A Murderous Art." *Critical Quarterly* 6 (1964):
355-63.

————. "Sea-Imagery in the Work of Sylvia Plath." In *The Art of Sylvia
Plath*, 91-99. Bloomington: Indiana University Press, 1970; London: Faber & Faber, 1970.

McCann, Janet. "Sylvia Plath's Bee Poems." *South and West* 14 (1978):
28-36.

McClatchy, J. D. "Staring From Her Hood of Bone: Adjusting to Sylvia
Plath." *American Poetry Since 1960*, edited by R. B Shaw, 155-66.
Oxford: Carcanet Press, 1973.

Maloff, Saul. "The Poet as Cult Goddess." *Commonweal* 103 (June 1976):
371-74.

Marcus, Jane. "Nostalgia is Not Enough: Why Elizabeth Hardwick Mis-
reads Ibsen, Plath, and Woolf." *Bucknell Review* 24 (1978): 157-77.

Martin, Wendy. " 'God's Lioness'—Sylvia Plath, Her Prose and Poetry."
Women's Studies: An Interdisciplinary Journal 1 (1973): 191-98.

Meissner, William. "The Rise of the Angel: Life Through Death in the
Poetry of Sylvia Plath." *Massachusetts Studies in English* 3 (Fall 1971):
34-39.

Melander, Ingrid. *The Poetry of Sylvia Plath: A Study of Themes*. Stock-
holm: Almquist & Wiksell, 1972 (Guthenburg Studies in English
No. 25).

Milford, Nancy. "The Journals of Sylvia Plath." *The New York Times
Book Review* (May 2, 1982): 1, 30-32.

Mollinger, Robert N. "A Symbolic Complex: Images of Death and Daddy
in the Poetry of Sylvia Plath." *Descant* 19 (Winter 1975): 45-52.

Moramarco, Fred. "Burned-Up Intensity: The Suicidal Poetry of Sylvia
Plath." *Mosaic* 15 (Winter 1982): 141-51.

Morris, Christopher. "Order and Chaos in Plath's 'The Colossus.' "
Concerning Poetry 15 (Fall 1982): 33-42.

Nance, Guinevara A., and Judith P. Jones. "Doing Away with Daddy:

Exorcism and Sympathetic Magic in Plath's Poetry." *Concerning Poetry* 11 (1978): 75-81.

Newman, Charles, ed. *The Art of Sylvia Plath: A Symposium*. Bloomington: Indiana University Press, 1970.

Oates, Joyce Carol. "The Death Throes of Romanticism: The Poems of Sylvia Plath." *Southern Review* 9 (July 1973): 501-22.

Oettle, Pamela. "Sylvia Plath's Last Poems." *Balcony* 3 (Spring 1965): 47-50.

Orr, Peter. *The Poet Speaks*. New York: Barnes and Noble, 1966, 167-72.

Ostriker, Alicia. " 'Face' as Style: The Americanization of Sylvia." *Language and Style* 1 (Summer 1968): 201-12.

Perloff, Marjorie. "Angst and Animism in the Poetry of Sylvia Plath." *Journal of Modern Literature* 1 (1970): 57-74.

———. "Extremist Poetry: Some Versions of the Sylvia Plath Myth." *Journal of Modern Literature* 2 (November 1972): 581-88.

———. "On the Road to Ariel: The 'Transitional' Poetry of Sylvia Plath." In *Sylvia Plath: The Woman and the Work*, edited by Edward Butscher, pp. 125-42. New York: Dodd, Mead, 1977.

———. " 'A Ritual for Being Born Twice': Sylvia Plath's *The Bell Jar*." *Contemporary Literature* 13 (Autumn 1972): 507-22.

Phillips, Robert. "The Dark Funnel: A Reading of Sylvia Plath." *Modern Poetry Studies* 3 (1972): 49-74.

Pollitt, Katha. "A Note of Triumph." *The Nation* 234 (January 1982): 52-55.

Pratt, Linda Ray. " 'The Spirit of Blackness Is In Us . . . ' " *Prairie Schooner* 47 (Spring 1973): 87-90.

Rapone, Anita. "The Body Is the Role: Sylvia Plath," In *Radical Feminism*, edited by Anne Koedt, Ellen Levine, and Anita Rapone, pp. 407-12. New York: Quadrangle Press, 1973.

Roland, Laurin K. "Sylvia Plath's 'Lesbos': A Self Divided." *Concerning Poetry* 9 (1976): 61-65.

Romano, John. "Sylvia Plath Reconsidered." *Commentary* 57 (April 1974): 47-52.

Rosen, Lois. "Sylvia Plath's Poetry about Children: A New Perspective." *Modern Poetry Studies* 10 (1981): 98-115.

Rosenblatt, Jon. "Sylvia Plath: The Drama of Initiation." *Twentieth Century Literature* 25 (1979): 21-36.

———. *Sylvia Plath: The Poetry of Initiation*. Chapel Hill: University of North Carolina Press, 1979.

Rosenstein, Harriet. "Reconsidering Sylvia Plath." *Ms. Magazine* 1 (September 1972): 44-51, 96-99.

Rosenthal, M. L. "Sylvia Plath and Confessional Poetry." In *The Art of Sylvia Plath*, edited by Charles Newman, pp. 69-76. Bloomington: Indiana University Press, 1970; London: Faber & Faber, 1970.

Salamon, Lynda B. " 'Double, Double': Perception in the Poetry of Sylvia Plath." *Spirit* 37 (1970): 34-39.

Sanazaro, Leonard. "James Joyce, T. S. Eliot, and Sylvia Plath." *Notes on Contemporary Literature* 11 (1981): 8-10.

———. " 'On the Decline of the Oracle, 1955-57: William James and Sylvia Plath's Dryad Poems." *Studia Mystica* 5 (Spring 1982): 59-70.

———. "Plath's 'Lady Lazarus.' " *Explicator* 41 (1983): 54-57.

———. "The Transfiguring Self: Sylvia Plath, a Reconsideration." *Centennial Review* 27 (Winter 1983): 62-74.

Scheerer, Constance. "The Deathly Paradise of Sylvia Plath." In *Sylvia Plath: The Woman and the Work*, edited by E. Butscher, pp. 166-76. New York: Dodd, 1977.

Sexton, Anne. "The Barfly Ought to Sing." In *The Art of Sylvia Plath*, edited by C. Newman. pp. 174-81. Bloomington: Indiana University Press, 1970; London: Faber & Faber, 1970.

Smith, Pamela. "Architectonics: Sylvia Plath's *Colossus*." In *Sylvia Plath: The Woman and the Work*, edited by E. Butscher. New York: Dodd, 1977.

———. "The Unitive Urge in the Poetry of Sylvia Plath." *New England Quarterly* 45 (September 1972): 323-39.

Spendal, R. J. "Sylvia Plath's 'Cut.' " *Modern Poetry Studies* 6 (Autumn 1975): 128-34.

Stainton, Rita T. "Vision and Voice in Three Poems by Sylvia Plath." *Windless Orchard* 17 (Spring 1974): 31-36.

Steiner, George. "Dying Is an Art." In *The Art of Sylvia Plath*, edited by Charles Newman, pp. 211-18. Bloomington: Indiana University Press, 1970; London: Faber & Faber, 1970.

———. "In Extremis." *Cambridge Review* 90 (February 1969): 247-49.

Steiner, Nancy Hunter. *A Closer Look at Ariel: A Memory of Sylvia Plath*. New York: Harper's Magazine Press, 1973.

Stewart, Penny. "Plath's Metaphors." *Explicator* 40 (Spring 1982): 59-60.

Storhoff, Gary P. "Plath's Comic Mode in 'You're.' " *Notes on Contemporary Literature* 9 (1979): 8-10.

Sumner, Nan McCowan. "Sylvia Plath." *Research Studies* 38 (June 1970): 112-21.

Talbot, Norman. "Sisterhood Is Powerful: The Moon in Sylvia Plath's Poetry." *New Poetry* 21 (June 1973): 23-26.

Taylor, Andrew. "Sylvia Plath's Mirror and Beehive." *Meanjin* 33 (September 1974): 256-65.

Taylor, Eleanor Ross. "Sylvia Plath's Last Poems." *Poetry* 89 (January 1967): 260-62.

Uroff, Margaret D. *Sylvia Plath and Ted Hughes*. Urbana: University of Illinois Press, 1979.

————. "Sylvia Plath on Motherhood." *Midwest Quarterly* 15 (October 1973): 70-90.

————. "Sylvia Plath's 'Tulips.' " *Paunch* 42-43 (December 1975): 90-96.

————. "Sylvia Plath's Women." *Concerning Poetry* 7 (1974): 45-56.

Van Dyne, Susan. "Fueling the Phoenix Fire: The Manuscripts of Sylvia Plath's 'Lady Lazarus.' *Massachusetts Review* 24 (Summer 1983): 395-410.

————. " 'More Terrible Than She Ever Was': The Manuscripts of Sylvia Plath's Bee Poems." In *Critical Essays on Sylvia Plath*, edited by Linda Wagner, pp. 154-70. Boston: G. K. Hall, 1984.

Vendler, Helen. "Crossing the Water." *The New York Review of Books* (October 10, 1971): 4, 48.

Wagner, Linda, ed. *Critical Essays on Sylvia Plath*. Boston: G. K. Hall, 1984.

————. "Plath's 'Ariel': 'Auspicious Gales.' " *Concerning Poetry* 10 (1977): 5-7.

Walsh, Thomas P., and Cameron Northouse. *Sylvia Plath and Anne Sexton: A Reference Guide*. Boston: G. K. Hall, 1974.

Wilhelm, Albert E. "Sylvia Plath's 'Metaphors.' " *Notes on Contemporary Literature* 10 (1980): 8-9.

Wood, David. "Art as Transcendence in Sylvia Plath's *Ariel*." *Kyushu American Literature* 23 (May 1982): 25-34.

Zajdel, Melody. "Apprenticed in a Bible of Dreams: Sylvia Plath's Short Stories." In *Critical Essays on Sylvia Plath*, edited by Linda Wagner, pp. 182-93. Boston: G. K. Hall, 1984.

Zivley, Sherry Lutz. "Plath's Family Album: Portraits of Grotesques." *Ball State University Forum* 20 (1979): 74-79.

Zollman, Sol. "Sylvia Plath and Imperialist Culture." *Literature and Ideology* 1 (1969): 11-22.

∿ Index ∿

NOTE: All items in quotes not otherwise identified are titles of Sylvia Plath's poems.

About the Author

PAMELA J. ANNAS is Associate Professor of English at the University of Massachusetts–Boston. She is the co-editor of *Literature and Society,* a member of the editorial collective of the journal *The Radical Teacher,* and the author of articles published in *Women's Studies, Women's Review of Books, Science Fiction Studies, College English, Colby Quarterly,* and several anthologies.